MW00978344

Meet the Apostles:
Biblical and Legendary Accounts
Robert C. Jones

Robert C. Jones
POB 1775
Kennesaw, GA 30156

robertcjones@mindspring.com

First Edition

ISBN: 1450535674
EAN-13: 9781450535670

This book is dedicated to the members of the "Christian History & Theology Courses" group on Facebook

Table of Contents

Introduction

All Christians are familiar with the fact that there were twelve original apostles. The names Peter, John, James, "Doubting Thomas", Judas Iscariot, etc. are household words. However, many Christians would be hard-pressed to name all twelve of the original apostles, impeded in part by the fact that at least two apostles have different names in different New Testament books. Even more difficult would be the task of naming the other people (excepting Paul) in the New Testament that have the word "apostle" associated with them. This book will look at all of the apostles mentioned in the New Testament, using "Biblical and Legendary Sources":

- **The New Testament**
- **Church Tradition** — Represented herein primarily from the *Ecclesiastical History* written by Church Father Eusebius around the time of the Council of Nicea in 325 A.D. Eusebius was the Bishop of Caesarea, and is best known for his list of "Accepted", "Rejected/Disputed", and "Impious/Absurd" New Testament-era books. A second source is the third century tract *On The Twelve Apostles - Where Each Of Them Preached, And Where He Met His End*, traditionally ascribed to the Church Father Hippolytus (170-236 A.D.)
- **Flavius Josephus** — from his *Jewish Antiquities* (written c. 93/94 A.D.)
- **Apocryphal** — Much of the "Christian Apocrypha" is made up of dubious "Acts" of the various apostles. While these are considered to be of no authority, they do capture some legends about the apostles that are still known today — and they may capture at least <u>some</u> authentic second and third century traditions about the apostles, such as where they preached.

Interestingly enough, Eusebius in his Church History records some early traditions about the apostles that also show up in the apocryphal "Acts". However, regarding the "Acts" themselves (and about apocryphal Gospels), Eusebius states:

...we have felt compelled to give this catalogue in order that we might be able to know both these works [generally accepted works] and those that are cited by the heretics under the name of the apostles, including, for instance, such books as the Gospels of Peter, of Thomas, of Matthias, or of any others besides them, and the Acts of Andrew and John and the other apostles, which no one belonging to the succession of ecclesiastical writers has deemed worthy of mention in his writings. And further, the character of the style is at variance with apostolic usage, and both the thoughts and the purpose of the things that are related in them are so completely out of accord with true orthodoxy that they clearly show themselves to be the fictions of heretics. Wherefore they are not to be placed even among the rejected writings, but are all of them to be cast aside as absurd and impious. (*The Church History of Eusebius*, Translated By the Rev. Arthur Cushman Mcgiffert, Ph.D., Book 3, Chapter 25[1])

Part One of this book will focus on "The Twelve" apostles chosen by Jesus. As a group, these apostles are mentioned in four lists in the New Testament:

Matt 10:2	Mark 3:16	Luke 6:14	Acts 1:13
Andrew	Andrew	Andrew	Andrew
Bartholomew	Bartholomew	Bartholomew	Bartholomew
James son of Alphaeus	James son of Alphaeus	James son of Alphaeus	James son of Alphaeus
James son of Zebedee	James son of Zebedee	James	James
John	John	John	John
Judas Iscariot	Judas Iscariot	Judas Iscariot	
Matthew	Matthew	Matthew	Matthew
Philip	Philip	Philip	Philip
Simon (who is called Peter)	Simon (to whom he gave the name Peter)	Simon (whom he named Peter)	Peter
Simon the Zealot	Simon the Zealot	Simon who was called the Zealot	Simon the Zealot
Thaddaeus	Thaddaeus	Judas son of James	Judas son of James
Thomas	Thomas	Thomas	Thomas

---

1   *The Nicene and Post-Nicene Fathers Second Series, Volume 1*, by Philip Schaff, editor

Part Two of this book focuses on apostles named in the New Testament outside of the Twelve, including Paul, James the Just (the brother of Jesus), Barnabas, Matthias, Andronicus and Junias (the last – Junias – provides us with some controversy).

New Testament figures such as Silas or Timothy are not included in this book, as the New Testament never associates the word "apostle" with them.

1847 print showing Jesus and the Twelve[2]

An appendix, *Leadership in the Early Church*, compares and contrasts the role of the apostles with other leaders, such as deacons, bishops and elders.

---

2   Library of Congress LC-DIG-ppmsca-17560

Part One – The Twelve

Chapter One – Andrew

Andrew, the brother of Simon Peter, was a Galilean fisherman. Originally from Bethsaida (John 1:44), at the time of the ministry of Jesus, he lived with his brother in a house near the Synagogue in Capernaum (Mark 1:29). Andrew was a follower of John the Baptist (John 1:35-40).

Matthew records that Jesus recruited Andrew and Peter while they were fishing in the Sea of Galilee (Matt 4:18-20). In the account in the Gospel of John (1:35-42), Andrew encounters Jesus first, and then rushes to tell his brother "We have found the Messiah".

Other appearances by Andrew in the New Testament include:
* Andrew was present when Jesus healed the fevered mother-in-law of Peter, and when Jesus began healing people from the house of Andrew and Peter in Capernaum (Mark 1:29-34).
* Andrew was with Peter, James, and John on the Mount of Olives when Jesus gave his sermon on the end times (Mark 13:3).
* Andrew finds the initial "five small barley loaves and two small fish" when Jesus feeds the 5,000 (John 6:8-9)
* Andrew is present with Jesus when a voice from heaven booms "I have glorified it, and will glorify it again." (John 12:20-30)

Church Tradition

According to Hippolytus:

> Andrew preached to the Scythians [modern day Georgia] and Thracians [modern day Bulgaria], and was crucified, suspended on an olive tree, at Patrae, a town of Achaia [Greece]; and there too he was buried. (*On the Twelve Apostles*, Hippolytus, Translated by A. Cleveland Coxe, D.D.[3])

According to Eusebius (Book 3, Chapter 1), Andrew's ministry was in Scythia.

---

3   *The Ante-Nicene Fathers Volume 5*, Edited by A. Roberts and J Donaldson

Apocryphal

The 3rd century *Acts And Martyrdom Of The Holy Apostle Andrew* describes the ministry and persecution of Andrew at Patrae, on the northwest coast of Achaia (modern-day Greece). The Acts are purported to have been written by "both presbyters and deacons of the churches of Achaia":

> WHAT we have all, both presbyters and deacons of the churches of Achaia, beheld with our eyes, we have written to all the churches established in the name of Christ Jesus, both in the east and west, north and south...This faith we have learned from the blessed Andrew, the apostle of our Lord Jesus Christ, whose passion also we, having seen it set forth before our eyes, have not hesitated to give an account of, according to the degree of ability we have. (*Acts and Martyrdom Of The Holy Apostle Andrew*, Translated By Alexander Walker, Esq.[4])

The Acts goes on to describe a debate between Andrew and the proconsul Aegeates, who wishes to have the mysteries of Christ revealed to him without accepting Christ and being baptized. Eventually, Aegeates has Andrew tortured and hung on a cross:

> And having thus spoken, the blessed Andrew, standing on the ground, and looking earnestly upon the cross, stripped himself and gave his clothes to the executioners, having urged the brethren that the executioners should come and do what had been commanded them; for they were standing at some distance. And they having come up, lifted him on the cross; and having stretched his body across with ropes, they only bound his feet, but did not sever his joints, having received this order from the proconsul: for he wished him to be in distress while hanging, and in the night-time, as he was suspended, to be eaten up alive by dogs. (*Acts and Martyrdom Of The Holy Apostle Andrew*, Translated By Alexander Walker, Esq.[5])

The end of Andrew is described:

> ... he became in the sight of all glad and exulting; for an exceeding splendor like lightning coming forth out of heaven shone down upon him, and so encircled him, that in consequence of such brightness mortal eyes could not look upon him at all. And the dazzling light remained about the space of half an hour. And when he had thus

---

4 *The Ante-Nicene Fathers Volume 8*, Edited by A. Roberts and J Donaldson
5 *Ibid*

spoken and glorified the Lord still more, the light withdrew itself, and he gave up the ghost, and along with the brightness itself he departed to the Lord in giving Him thanks. (*Acts and Martyrdom Of The Holy Apostle Andrew*, Translated By Alexander Walker, Esq.[6])

In the somewhat more lurid *Acts Of Andrew And Matthias In The City Of The Man-Eaters*, Andrew is carried by angels to rescue Matthias, who has been imprisoned by cannibals. In one paragraph, Andrew is depicted raising people from the dead, baptizing them, and building a church:

Then the holy Andrew ordered to be brought up all who had died in the water. And they were not able to bring them; for there had died a great multitude both of men, and women, and children, and cattle. Then Andrew prayed, and they all came to life. And after these things he drew a plan of a church, and he caused the church to be built. And he baptized them, and gave them the ordinances of our Lord Jesus Christ, saying to them: Stand by these, in order that you may know the mysteries of our Lord Jesus Christ. (*Acts of Andrew and Matthias*, Translated By Alexander Walker, Esq.[7])

---

6 *Ibid*
7 *Ibid*

Chapter Two – Bartholomew/Nathanael

While Bartholomew is mentioned in all four lists of apostles in the New Testament, he is not mentioned in any other context. The name means simply "son of Talmai", so he may have had a personal name. This personal name may have been Nathanael, mentioned several times in the Gospel of John.

If Nathanael is equated with Bartholomew, we have at least a few characteristics about this enigmatic apostle. In the first chapter of the Gospel of John (John 1:45-51), Philip goes to find Nathanael (the names Philip and Bartholomew always follow each other in the Synoptic Gospel lists) and tell him "We have found the one Moses wrote about in the Law, and about whom the prophets also wrote--Jesus of Nazareth, the son of Joseph." (John 1:45, NIV). Nathanael makes the famous reply "Nazareth! Can anything good come from there?" (John 1:46, NIV).

Evidently, though, Nathanael has a good heart, as Jesus says about him "Here is a true Israelite, in whom there is nothing false." (John 1:47, NIV). Nathanael has the distinction of being the first apostle to declare that Jesus was both the Son of God and the King of Israel. (John 1:49, NIV)

Nathanael is present at the third post-resurrection meeting of Jesus with the Apostles (John 21:1-14), by the Sea of Galilee. The incident involves a miraculous catch of fish (John tells us 153), and a fish fry on the beach involving Jesus and his disciples. In the passage, we are told that Nathanael is from Cana in Galilee. We may infer that he is a fisherman by trade.

Church Tradition

According to Hippolytus, Bartholomew preached in India:

> Bartholomew, again, preached to the Indians, to whom he also gave the Gospel according to Matthew, and was crucified with his head downward, and was buried in Allanum, a town of the great Armenia

[modern day southern Georgia]. (*On the Twelve Apostles*, Hippolytus, Translated by A. Cleveland Coxe, D.D.[8])

Eusebius, in his Church History, confirms the ministry of Bartholomew in India, and adds an eye witness account:

> ABOUT that time, Pantaenus, a man highly distinguished for his learning, had charge of the school of the faithful in Alexandria... Pantaenus...is said to have gone to India. It is reported that among persons there who knew of Christ, he found the Gospel according to Matthew, which had anticipated his own arrival. For Bartholomew, one of the apostles, had preached to them, and left with them the writing of Matthew in the Hebrew language, which they had preserved till that time. (*The Church History of Eusebius*, Translated By the Rev. Arthur Cushman Mcgiffert, Ph.D., Book 5, Chapter 10[9])

Apocryphal

In the *Martyrdom Of The Holy And Glorious Apostle Bartholomew*, Bartholomew preaches in India, and becomes actively involved in casting out demons. One demon describes him as follows (perhaps not a very trustworthy source!):

> He has black hair, a shaggy head, a fair skin, large eyes, beautiful nostrils, his ears hidden by the hair of his head, with a yellow beard, a few gray hairs, of middle height, and neither tall nor stunted, but middling, clothed with a white undercloak bordered with purple, and upon his shoulders a very white cloak; and his clothes have been worn twenty-six years, but neither are they dirty, nor have they waxed old. Seven times a day he bends the knee to the Lord, and seven times a night does he pray to God. His voice is like the sonnet of a strong trumpet; there go along with him angels of God, who allow him neither to be weary, nor to hunger, nor to thirst; his face, and his soul, and his heart are always glad and rejoicing; he foresees everything, he knows and speaks every tongue of every nation. (*Martyrdom Of The Holy And Glorious Apostle Bartholomew*, Translated By Alexander Walker, Esq.[10])

---

8   *The Ante-Nicene Fathers Volume 5*, Edited by A. Roberts and J Donaldson
9   *The Nicene and Post-Nicene Fathers Second Series, Volume 1*, by Philip Schaff, editor
10 *The Ante-Nicene Fathers Volume 8*, Edited by A. Roberts and J Donaldson

In the course of a long sermon on the basic tenets of the Gospels to King Polymius, (whose daughter was exorcised of a demon by Bartholomew), the Apostle gives this brief description of his calling:

> And when the Lord had conquered the tyrant [Satan], He sent His apostles into all the world, that He might redeem His people from the deception of the devil; and one of these I am, an apostle of Christ. (*Martyrdom Of The Holy And Glorious Apostle Bartholomew*, Translated By Alexander Walker, Esq.[11])

After King Polymius converts to Christianity, his brother King Astreges is enraged, and orders Bartholomew beheaded:

> Then the king...ordered the holy apostle Bartholomew to be beaten with rods; and after having been thus scourged, to be beheaded.

> And innumerable multitudes came from all the cities, to the number of twelve thousand, who had believed in him along with the king; and they took up the remains of the apostle with singing of praise and with all glory, and they laid them in the royal tomb, and glorified God. And the king Astreges having heard of this, ordered him to be thrown into the sea; and his remains were carried into the island of Liparis. (*Martyrdom Of The Holy And Glorious Apostle Bartholomew*, Translated By Alexander Walker, Esq.[12])

King Astreges soon dies a horrible death, and his brother Polymius becomes bishop, and rules for 20 years.

Other Legends

Other legends say that Bartholomew was flayed alive in Armenia. His remains are said to be, variously, in Rome and in Canterbury Cathedral in England.

---

11 *Ibid*
12 *Ibid*

Chapter Three - James, Son of Alphaeus

We have almost no canonical information about James, Son of Alphaeus, other than that he appears on all four New Testament apostolic lists. Mark 2:14 identifies that Levi/Matthew the tax collect- or also had a father named Alphaeus, so the two may have been brothers or half brothers.

Some scholars have linked the "James the younger" in Mark 15:40 with James, son of Alphaeus. If this identification is true, then James had a mother named Mary that was present at the crucifixion, and a brother named Joses.

Church Tradition

Hippolytus identifies that James was stoned to death in Jerusalem:

> And James the son of Alphaeus, when preaching in Jerusalem, was stoned to death by the Jews, and was buried there beside the temple. (*On the Twelve Apostles,* Hippolytus, Translated by A. Cleveland Coxe, D.D.[13])

Eusebius doesn't mention James in his Church History.

---

13 *The Ante-Nicene Fathers Volume 5*, Edited by A. Roberts and J Donaldson

Chapter Four - James, Son of Zebedee

James, son of Zebedee and brother of John is mentioned in all four New Testament apostolic lists. The calling of James (and his brother) is recorded in Matthew:

> Going on from there, he saw two other brothers, James son of Zebedee and his brother John. They were in a boat with their father Zebedee, preparing their nets. Jesus called them, and immediately they left the boat and their father and followed him. (Matthew 4:21-22, NIV)

Thus, we know that James was a fisherman, and that he worked with his father. In Luke 5:10, James and John are identified as Peter's partners in the fishing business. Mark 1:20 indicates that the Zebedee family had hired men in the fishing business, perhaps indicating that James and his brother came from a successful family business. Mathew 27:55-56 identifies that the mother of James and John was a follower of Jesus, and was present at his crucifixion.

James and his brother (along with Peter) are traditionally identified as being part of the "inner circle" of the apostles of Jesus, because they were present at several key events that the other apostles were not. These events included:

The transfiguration	Matt 17:1, Mark 9:2, Luke 9:29
The raising of the daughter of Jairus from the dead	Mark 5:35-43, Luke 8:49-56
Present at the mini-apocalypse, delivered by Jesus on the Mount of Olives	Mark 13:3
With Jesus during his agony in the Garden of Gethsemane	Mark 14:32-42, Matt 26:36-46

During the description of the raising of the daughter of Jairus from the dead, the existence of inner circle is clearly outlined:

> He [Jesus] did not let anyone follow him except Peter, James and John the brother of James. (Mark 5:37, NIV)

The inner circle is also present at a miraculous catch of fish on the Sea of Galilee (Luke 5:1-11). The brothers were also present when the resurrected Jesus fried fish for some of the apostles on the shores of the Sea of Galilee, as described in John 21.

19th century engraving showing the "inner circle" (left) present when Jesus raises the daughter of Jarus from the dead[14]

Mark 3:17 identifies that James and his brother had the nickname "Sons of Thunder", which may apply to their temper or their impetuousness. This temper is exhibited in Luke 9:51-56 when James and John are affronted because a Samaritan village is not interested in hearing Jesus preach:

> When the disciples James and John saw this, they asked, "Lord, do you want us to call fire down from heaven to destroy them?" (Luke 9:54, NIV)

---

14 Library of Congress LC-DIG-pga-04101

Their impetuousness is demonstrated in Mark 10:35-41, when James and John ask Jesus "Let one of us sit at your right and the other at your left in your glory." The other apostles become indignant at this presumptuousness (Mark 10:41).

Post-Pentecostal

James holds the distinction of being the only apostle in the New Testament that has his martyrdom recorded in the Scriptures:

> It was about this time that King Herod arrested some who belonged to the church, intending to persecute them. He had James, the brother of John, put to death with the sword. (Acts 12:1-2, NIV)

Paul, in his letter to the Galatians, reports that James supported his ministry to the Gentiles:

> James, Peter and John, those reputed to be pillars, gave me and Barnabas the right hand of fellowship when they recognized the grace given to me. They agreed that we should go to the Gentiles, and they to the Jews. (Galatians 2:9, NIV)

This would tend to indicate that James the "pillar" had an important place in the post-Pentecostal church.

Church Tradition

According to Hippolytus:

> James, his brother, when preaching in Judea, was cut off with the sword by Herod the tetrarch, and was buried there. (*On the Twelve Apostles*, Hippolytus, Translated by A. Cleveland Coxe, D.D.[15])

According to Eusebius, James was beheaded:

> First Stephen was stoned to death by them, and after him James, the son of Zebedee and the brother of John, was beheaded... (*The Church History of Eusebius*, Translated By the Rev. Arthur Cushman Mcgiffert, Ph.D., Book 3, Chapter 5[16])

---

15 *The Ante-Nicene Fathers Volume 5*, Edited by A. Roberts and J Donaldson

"The Apostle James (the major) beheaded in Jerusalem, A.D. 45"[17]

Eusebius also records another tradition regarding the death of James:

> And concerning this James, Clement, in the seventh book of his Hypo-
> typoses, relates a story which is worthy of mention; telling it as he re-
> ceived it from those who had lived before him. He says that the one
> who led James to the judgment-seat, when he saw him bearing his
> testimony, was moved, and confessed that he was himself also a
> Christian. They were both therefore, he says, led away together; and
> on the way he begged James to forgive him. And he, after considering
> a little, said, "Peace be with thee," and kissed him. And thus they
> were both beheaded at the same time. (*The Church History of Eusebi-
> us*, Translated By the Rev. Arthur Cushman Mcgiffert, Ph.D., Book 2,
> Chapter 9[18])

---

16 *The Nicene and Post-Nicene Fathers Second Series, Volume 1*, by Philip Schaff,
   editor
17 *Martyrs Mirror*, by Thieleman J. van Braght, 1660
18 *Ibid*

Other Legends

Medieval tradition associates James with a ministry in Spain. Other Medieval legends claim that his remains were brought to Santiago de Compostela in northwest Spain. His head is also said to rest in a 12th century Armenian Church in Jerusalem.

Chapter Five – John

John on Patmos (Photo by Robert Jones)[19]

John, brother of James and son of Zebedee, is named in all four New Testament apostolic lists. Much of what has already been said about his brother James is also true for John, which is summarized here:

- John was a Galilean fisherman who worked with his father and brother. He was called by Jesus with his brother James. (Matthew 4:21/22). In Luke 5:10, John and his brother are identified as Peter's partners in the fishing business.
- As noted before, John and his brother are traditionally identified as being part of the "inner circle" of the apostles of Jesus, because they were present at several key events that the other apostles were not. These events included:

---

19 From a stain glass window in the Cathedral of the Plains, Victoria, Kansas

The transfiguration	Matt 17:1, Mark 9:2, Luke 9:29
The raising of the daughter of Jairus from the dead	Mark 5:35-43, Luke 8:49-56
Present at the mini-apocalypse, delivered by Jesus on the Mount of Olives	Mark 13:3
With Jesus during his agony in the Garden of Gethsemane	Mark 14:32-42, Matt 26:36-46

Ancient olive tree in the Garden of Gethsemene (Photo by Barbara Brim)

Also, John and his brother were present when Jesus healed the fever-ridden mother-in-law of Peter (Mark 1:29-31), and when when Jesus causes a miraculous catch of fish on the Sea of Galilee (Luke 5:1-11).

- In Mark 10, John and James incur the displeasure of the other apostles when they ask Jesus, "Let one of us sit at your right and the other at your left in your glory." (Mark 10:35-39)
- Mathew 27:55-56 identifies that the mother of John and James was a follower of Jesus, and was present at his crucifixion

- Mark 3:17 identifies that James and his brother had the nickname "Sons of Thunder", which may apply to their temper (see Luke 9:51-56)

John is also mentioned several times apart from his brother in the Gospels:

- John is mildly rebuked by Jesus in Luke 9:49-50 after John complains about a man "driving out demons in your name"
- In Luke 22:7-13, John (along with Peter) is given the important task of preparing the logistics for the Last Supper

John is not mentioned by name in the Gospel of John. Church tradition (more on this later) identifies John with the "disciple that Jesus loved" that is mentioned five times in the Gospel of John:

Reference	Verse(s)
During the Last Supper, this disciple is asked by Peter who is going to betray Jesus	John 13:23-26
The disciple is given the responsibility of taking care of Mary, Mother of Jesus	John 19:26-27
With Peter, the disciple is told by Mary Magdalene that the tomb is empty	John 20:1-9
The disciple is the first one to identify Jesus at the miraculous catch of fish after the resurrection	John 21:1-14
Jesus seems to indicate that this disciple will outlive Peter	John 21:20-24

The miraculous catch of fish (Photo by Robert Jones)[20]

Post-Pentecostal

In Acts, John is depicted as a close associate of Peter, and is involved in the early preaching and healing activities:

Reference	Verse(s)
Healing a cripple	Acts 3:1-10
Peter and John are jailed by the Sanhedrin, and released after being admonished to no longer teach about Jesus	Acts 4:1-22
Peter and John preach in Samaria, baptizing through the laying on of hands	Acts 8:14-17

Like his brother James, John is referred to as a "pillar" of the church in Galatians 2:9. Paul notes that he supported the Pauline ministry to the Gentiles.

---

20 From a stained glass window at Mars Hill Presbyterian Church, Acworth, GA

Church Tradition

There are many strong church traditions regarding John. As early as c. 180 A.D., Irenaeus (Bishop of Lyons from 177-202 A.D.) says that John was the author of the Gospel of John:

> ...John, the disciple of the Lord, who also had leaned upon His breast, did himself publish a Gospel during his residence at Ephesus in Asia. (*Against Heresies*, Irenaeus, Translated by A. Cleveland Coxe, D.D., Book 3, Chapter 1[21])

Eusebius discusses the reason that John wrote his Gospel:

> Matthew and John have left us written memorials, and they, tradition says, were led to write only under the pressure of necessity...And when Mark and Luke had already published their Gospels, they say that John, who had employed all his time in proclaiming the Gospel orally, finally proceeded to write for the following reason. The three Gospels already mentioned having come into the hands of all and into his own too, they say that he accepted them and bore witness to their truthfulness; but that there was lacking in them an account of the deeds done by Christ at the beginning of his ministry. (*The Church History of Eusebius*, Translated By the Rev. Arthur Cushman Mcgiffert, Ph.D., Book 3, Chapter 24[22])

By tradition, John was also the author of three canonical letters, and the Apocalypse. Eusebius was pretty sure about John I, less sure about John II, III, and Revelation:

> But of the writings of John, not only his Gospel, but also the former of his epistles, has been accepted without dispute both now and in ancient times. But the other two are disputed. In regard to the Apocalypse, the opinions of most men are still divided. But at the proper time this question likewise shall be decided from the testimony of the ancients. (*The Church History of Eusebius*, Translated By the Rev. Arthur Cushman Mcgiffert, Ph.D., Book 3, Chapter 24[23])

---

21 *The Ante-Nicene Fathers Volume 1*, Edited by A. Roberts and J Donaldson
22 *The Nicene and Post-Nicene Fathers Second Series, Volume 1*, by Philip Schaff, editor
23 *Ibid*

However, all three epistles, and the Apocalypse, were firmly entrenched in the New Testament canon by 367 A.D., and have remained there ever since.

According to Hippolytus, John was banished by Domitian to the Isle of Patmos, and later died in Ephesus:

> John, again, in Asia, was banished by Domitian the king to the isle of Patmos, in which also he wrote his Gospel and saw the apocalyptic vision; and in Trajan's time he fell asleep at Ephesus, where his remains were sought for, but could not be found. (*On the Twelve Apostles*, Hippolytus, Translated by A. Cleveland Coxe, D.D.[24])

The traditions connecting John with Ephesus and Patmos are well established. Eusebius records:

> ...Asia to John, who, after he had lived some time there, died at Ephesus. (*The Church History of Eusebius*, Translated By the Rev. Arthur Cushman Mcgiffert, Ph.D., Book 3, Chapter 1[25])

> IT is said that in this persecution [Domitian] the apostle and evangelist John, who was still alive, was condemned to dwell on the island of Patmos in consequence of his testimony to the divine word. (*The Church History of Eusebius*, Translated By the Rev. Arthur Cushman Mcgiffert, Ph.D., Book 3, Chapter 17[26])

Eusebius also records that John outlived Domitian:

> AT that time the apostle and evangelist John, the one whom Jesus loved, was still living in Asia, and governing the churches of that region, having returned after the death of Domitian from his exile on the island... [Irenaeus] in the second book of his work Against Heresies, writes as follows: "And all the elders that associated with John the disciple of the Lord in Asia bear witness that John delivered it to them. For he remained among them until the time of Trajan." (*The Church History of Eusebius*, Translated By the Rev. Arthur Cushman Mcgiffert, Ph.D., Book 3, Chapter 23[27])

---

24 *The Ante-Nicene Fathers Volume 5*, Edited by A. Roberts and J Donaldson
25 *The Nicene and Post-Nicene Fathers Second Series, Volume 1*, by Philip Schaff, editor
26 *Ibid*
27 *Ibid*

The emperor Domitian began his rule in 81 A.D., and died in 96 A.D. This would mean that John would have been in his 80s or 90s when he died.

Eusebius also records the words of Clement of Alexandria regarding the preaching and establishment of churches in Asia by John:

> For when, after the tyrant's death, he returned from the isle of Patmos to Ephesus, he went away upon their invitation to the neighboring territories of the Gentiles, to appoint bishops in some places, in other places to set in order whole churches, elsewhere to choose to the ministry some one of those that were pointed out by the Spirit... (*The Church History of Eusebius*, Translated By the Rev. Arthur Cushman Mcgiffert, Ph.D., Book 3, Chapter 23[28])

Eusebius also records a tradition regarding the death of John:

> The time, of John's death has also been given in a general way, but his burial place is indicated by an epistle of Polycrates (who was bishop of the parish of Ephesus), addressed to Victor, bishop of Rome. In this epistle he mentions him together with the apostle Philip and his daughters in the following words: "For in Asia also great lights have fallen asleep, which shall rise again on the last day, at the coming of the Lord, when he shall come with glory from heaven and shall seek out all the saints. Among these are...John, who was both a witness and a teacher, who reclined upon the bosom of the Lord, and being a priest wore the sacerdotal plate. He also sleeps at Ephesus. (*The Church History of Eusebius*, Translated By the Rev. Arthur Cushman Mcgiffert, Ph.D.[29])

Finally, Eusebius records a tradition from Appollonius that John raised a man from the dead:

> He [Apollonius]...relates that a dead man had, through the Divine power, been raised by John himself in Ephesus. (*The Church History of Eusebius*, Translated By the Rev. Arthur Cushman Mcgiffert, Ph.D., Book 5, Chapter 19[30])

---

28 *Ibid*
29 *Ibid*
30 *Ibid*

Apocryphal

In the *Acts Of The Holy Apostle And Evangelist John The Theologian*, John is seized on order of Domitian and brought before him. John drinks poison to prove that Jesus and the Holy Spirit protect him. Then a condemned prisoner is made to drink the poison to prove that it is lethal. The prisoner dies, and John promptly raises him from the dead. John is eventually banished to Patmos:

> Domitian, astonished at all the wonders, sent him away to an island, appointing for him a set time.
>
> And straightway John sailed to Patmos, where also he was deemed worthy to see the revelation of the end. And when Domitian was dead, Nerva succeeded to the kingdom, and recalled all who had been banished; and having kept the kingdom for a year, he made Trajan his successor in the kingdom. And when he was king over the Romans, John went to Ephesus, and regulated all the teaching of the church, holding many conferences, and reminding them of what the Lord had said to them, and what duty he had assigned to each. And when he was old and changed, he ordered Polycarp to be bishop over the church. (*Acts Of The Holy Apostle And Evangelist John The Theologian*, Translated By Alexander Walker, Esq.[31])

In this account, there is some doubt cast as to whether John really died:

> And gazing towards heaven, he glorified God; and having sealed himself altogether, he stood and said to us, Peace and grace be with you, brethren! and sent the brethren away. And when they went on the morrow they did not find him, but his sandals, and a fountain welling up. And after that they remembered what had been said to Peter by the Lord about him: For what does it concern thee if I should wish him to remain until I come? And they glorified God for the miracle that had happened. And having thus believed, they retired praising and blessing the benignant God; because to Him is due glory now and ever, and to ages of ages. Amen. (*Acts Of The Holy Apostle And Evangelist John The Theologian*, Translated By Alexander Walker, Esq.[32])

---

31 *The Ante-Nicene Fathers Volume 8*, Edited by A. Roberts and J Donaldson
32 *Ibid*

Chapter Six - Judas Iscariot

Judas fleeing from the Last Supper[33]

Judas Iscariot is the most reviled figure in the New Testament - Jesus actually refers to him as a devil in John 6:70-71. He betrayed Jesus to the Sanhedrin for 30 pieces of silver.

Judas was the son of Simon Iscariot (John 6:71). "Iscariot" is variously interpreted as meaning "dagger-man" (i.e. that Judas was a Zealot), or "man of Kerioth", a town near Hebron. If the latter is correct, then Judas was the only non-Galilean among the twelve – an outsider from the beginning.

---

33 Library of Congress LC-USZ62-137485

Judas is mentioned in the three Synoptic Gospel lists of the apostles. He is, of course, omitted from the list in Acts.

The betrayal

The betrayal by Judas is mentioned starkly in Matthew:

> Then one of the Twelve--the one called Judas Iscariot--went to the chief priests and asked, "What are you willing to give me if I hand him over to you?" So they counted out for him thirty silver coins. From then on Judas watched for an opportunity to hand him over. (Matthew 26:14-16, NIV)

Luke 22:3 records that Satan entered Judas before he made his deal with the chief priests.

The Last Supper – the traitor identified

In Matthew 26:20-25, Jesus discusses the fact that he will be betrayed by one of the twelve, and that "It would be better for him if he had not been born." When Judas asks "Surely not I, Rabbi?" Jesus answered, "Yes, it is you."

The Last Supper[34]

34 Library of Congress LC-USZC4-6873

John 13:27 identifies that Satan entered into Judas at the Last Supper.

The role of Judas in the capture of Jesus

The actual capture of Jesus is variously described in the Gospels:

Reference	Verse(s)
"Judas said, 'Greetings, Rabbi!' and kissed him."	Matthew 26:46-50
"With him was a crowd armed with swords and clubs"	Mark 14:43-46
"Judas, are you betraying the Son of Man with a kiss?"	Luke 22:47-48
"And Judas the traitor was standing there with them."	John 18:1-5

Character of Judas

The Gospel of John is especially harsh in its characterization of Judas. In the following passage (which also tells us that Judas was the treasurer of the apostles), Judas is referred to as a thief:

> He did not say this because he cared about the poor but because he was a thief; as keeper of the money bag, he used to help himself to what was put into it. (John 12:6, NIV)

Matthew 27:34 records that Judas felt remorse after turning Jesus over to his enemies ("'I have sinned,' he said, 'for I have betrayed innocent blood.'")

Death of Judas

The New Testament offers two versions (not necessarily contradictory) of the death of Judas. Matthew 27:5 records that Judas committed suicide by hanging. Acts gives a somewhat more graphic description of the death of Judas:

> (With the reward he got for his wickedness, Judas bought a field; there he fell headlong, his body burst open and all his intestines spilled out. Everyone in Jerusalem heard about this, so they called that field in their language *Akeldama*, that is, Field of Blood. (Acts 1:18-19, NIV)

Judas and predestination

The life and death of Judas Iscariot is often used as an example of pre-destination. Both Jesus (John 13:18) and Peter (Acts 1:15-20) speak of the traitorous actions of Judas as being in fulfillment of the Scriptures (Psalms 41:9), and Peter says that his end was also foretold by the prophets (Psalms 69:25, 109:8).

Chapter Seven – Matthew/Levi

Matthew appears in all four apostolic lists in the New Testament. Mark and Luke also refer to him as "Levi". Mark 2:14 identifies Matthew (Levi) as the "son of Alphaeus", so Matthew may have been related to James, son of Alphaeus (brother or half-brother).

Matthew was a tax collector (Matt 9:9) – a singularly unpopular occupation in 1st century Palestine! All three synoptic Gospels report that Jesus attended a dinner at the house of Matthew. The version in Luke 5:27-32 identifies that the dinner was held in honor of Jesus by Matthew – "Then Levi held a great banquet for Jesus at his house..."

Luke 5:28 tells us that Levi "left everything" to follow Jesus.

Church Tradition

While the Gospel of Matthew bears no author attribution in the text, very early church tradition identifies the Gospel with Matthew. Bishop Papias of Hierapolis, as early as c. 110 A.D., stated:

> Matthew put together the oracles [of the Lord] in the Hebrew language, and each one interpreted them as best he could. (*The Church History of Eusebius*, Translated By the Rev. Arthur Cushman Mcgiffert, Ph.D., Book 3, Chapter 39[35])

According to Hippolytus:

> And Matthew wrote the Gospel in the Hebrew tongue, and published it at Jerusalem, and fell asleep at Hierees, a town of Parthia. [Parthia is near modern day Tehran] (*On the Twelve Apostles*, Hippolytus, Translated by A. Cleveland Coxe, D.D.[36])

Apocryphal

In the apocryphal *Acts And Martyrdom Of St. Matthew The Apostle*, Jesus (appearing in the form of a child) sends Matthew to "Myrna, the city of the man-eaters". After casting out demons from the wife, son,

---

35 *The Nicene and Post-Nicene Fathers Second Series, Volume 1*, by Philip Schaff, editor
36 *The Ante-Nicene Fathers Volume 5*, Edited by A. Roberts and J Donaldson

and daughter-in-law of the King Fulvanus, the king becomes jealous because they want to spend all of their time with Matthew. The King several times tries to burn Matthew to death, but Matthew is protected by Jesus. In time, the fire used to try to burn Matthew burns up most of the King's kingdom. Matthew eventually dies, and ascends to heaven:

> ...we all saw Matthew rising up, as it were, from the bed, and going into heaven, led by the hand by a beautiful boy; and twelve men in shining garments came to meet him, having never-fading and golden crowns on their head; and we saw how that child crowned Matthew, so as to be like them, and in a flash of lightning they went away to heaven. (*Acts And Martyrdom Of St. Matthew The Apostle*, Translated By Alexander Walker, Esq.[37])

Eventually the king converts to Christianity, and becomes Bishop of his land. The Acts end with the following:

> And Saint Matthew finished his course in the country of the man-eaters, in the city of Myrna, on the sixteenth of the month of November, our Lord Jesus Christ reigning, to whom be glory and strength, now and ever, and to ages of ages. Amen. (*Acts And Martyrdom Of St. Matthew The Apostle*, Translated By Alexander Walker, Esq.[38])

Other traditions record his martyrdom in Ethiopia and in Persia.

An apocryphal Gospel is also attributed to Matthew, that purports to tell about the "birth of the Virgin Mary, and the nativity and infancy of our Lord Jesus Christ".

---

37 *The Ante-Nicene Fathers Volume 8*, Edited by A. Roberts and J Donaldson
38 *Ibid*

Chapter Eight – Peter

Peter, with the keys to the Kingdom (Photo by Robert Jones)[39]

Simon Peter, along with his brother Andrew, was a Galilean fisherman. According to Luke 5:3, he owned a boat. Peter and his brother were originally from the town of Bethsaida (John 1:44), but were living in Capernaum at the time of the ministry of Jesus. It appears that Jesus sometimes used the house of Simon and Andrew as a base of operations in Capernaum (Mark 1:32-34, Luke 4:40-43).

Simon Peter is mentioned in all four apostolic lists in the New Testament. John 1:42 identifies that Jesus gave Simon the name "Cephas", or Peter (which means "rock").

---

39 From a stain glass window in the Cathedral of the Plains, Victoria, Kansas

Peter was the son of Jonah (Matt 16:17). He was married - 1 Cor 9:5 records that Peter took his wife on some of his missionary journeys. Peter's mother-in-law was healed by Jesus of a fever (Mark 1:29-31, Luke 4:38-39).

Calling of Peter

According to the account in Matthew, Andrew and Peter were the first apostles selected by Jesus who tells them in Mat 4:19 "Come, follow me and I will make you fishers of men." (Also, Mark 1:16-17) In Luke 5:1-11, the calling of Peter is associated with a miraculous catch of fish, which causes a frightened Peter to say "Go away from me, Lord; I am a sinful man!"

A somewhat different account in John 1:41-42, depicts that Simon is brought to Jesus by his brother Andrew. John 1 also indicates that Peter may have been a follower of John the Baptist (John 1:35-40).

Peter is given an especially important role in the Gospel of Matthew when he is the first one of the apostles to proclaim that Jesus is the messiah and the Son of God:

> "But what about you?" he asked. "Who do you say I am?" Simon Peter answered, "You are the Christ, the Son of the living God." Jesus replied, "Blessed are you, Simon son of Jonah, for this was not revealed to you by man, but by my Father in heaven." (Matthew 16:15-17, NIV)

The "inner circle"

Peter was part of the "inner circle" of the apostles of Jesus, along with the brothers James and John. They were involved in several key events that the other apostles weren't privy to:

The transfiguration	Matt 17:1, Mark 9:2, Luke 9:29
The raising of the daughter of Jairus from the dead	Mark 5:35-43, Luke 8:49-56
Present at the mini-apocalypse, delivered by Jesus on the Mount of Olives	Mark 13:3
With Jesus during his agony in the Garden of Gethsemane	Mark 14:32-42, Matt 26:36-46

Along with John, Peter is asked by Jesus to make preparations for the Last Supper	Luke 22:8-13

Character and characteristics

Peter is especially endearing as an "everyman", demonstrating his innate practicality when, during the transfiguration, he seems more focused on building some sort of condominiums for Jesus, Moses, and Elijah, than on the significance of the two prophets appearing with Jesus:

> As the men were leaving Jesus, Peter said to him, "Master, it is good for us to be here. Let us put up three shelters--one for you, one for Moses and one for Elijah." (He did not know what he was saying.) (Luke 9:33, NIV)

Peter is often depicted as having dialogues with the Savior. In these dialogues, Peter is portrayed variously as being impetuous, practical, inquiring, enthusiastic, and sometimes even a little slow. On several occasions, Jesus rebukes him.

Reference	Verse(s)
The Temple Tax	Matt 17:24-27
"I tell you, not seven times, but seventy-seven times."	Matt 18:21-22
"The fig tree you cursed has withered!"	Mark 11:20-25
"Lord, to whom shall we go? You have the words of eternal life."	John 6:67-70
"Are you still so dull?"	Matthew 15:15-16
Peter asked, "Lord, are you telling this parable to us, or to everyone?"	Luke 12:35-48
"No," said Peter, "you shall never wash my feet."	John 13:6-9
As soon as Simon Peter heard him say, "It is the Lord," he wrapped his outer garment around him (for he had taken it off) and jumped into the water.	John 21:7
"Out of my sight, Satan!"	Matthew 16:21-23, Mark 8:32-33
"Put your sword away! Shall I not drink the cup the Father has given me?"	John 18:10-11

1867 print showing Jesus washing the feet of the apostles[40]

Prior to Pentecost, Peter is portrayed as a man that wants to have faith, but cannot always maintain it. Matthew 14:25-33 is an example, with Peter believing he can walk on water, but then losing faith because of the strong wind. In Matthew 26:33-35, after Jesus has announced that he will be betrayed, Peter claims "Even if all fall away on account of you, I never will." Jesus knows better, though, and replies "...before the rooster crows, you will disown me three times." (Also, Mark 14:29-31, Luke 22:33-34). Of course, Peter goes on to disown the Lord three times (once given away by his Galilean accent) (Matt 26:69-75; see also Mark 14:66-72, Luke 22:54-62, John 18:15-27).

1867 print showing Jesus walking on water[41]

Post-resurrection

Peter appears in several key scenes after the resurrection. In Mark 16:1-8, Mary Magdalene, Mary the mother of James, and Salome are told by a young man dressed in white to "tell his disciples and Peter" that Jesus will see them in Galilee. Some people interpret this to mean that, after disowning Christ three times, Peter is temporarily not considered to be one of the Apostles. In John 21:15-17, Peter is prompted by Jesus to tell him that he loves him three times.

In Luke 24:12 and John 20:1-9, Peter is depicted as viewing the empty tomb. A mysterious reference in Luke 24:34 and 1 Cor 15:5 identifies that Peter was the first apostle to whom the risen Lord appeared. However, there is no other New Testament record of this event.

Along with several other apostles, Simon Peter is present at the miraculous post-resurrection fish catch/fry, depicted in John 21:1-14.

Death of Peter prefigured

Later Church tradition (see section below) says that Peter met his death by crucifixion under Nero. An eerie set of passages at the end of the Gospel of John seems to prefigure his death (John lived long after Peter, and very likely would have known the details of his death):

---

41 Library of Congress LC-DIG-pga-02626

Simon Peter asked him, "Lord, where are you going?" Jesus replied, "Where I am going, you cannot follow now, but you will follow later." (John 13:36, NIV)

"I tell you the truth, when you were younger you dressed yourself and went where you wanted; but when you are old you will stretch out your hands, and someone else will dress you and lead you where you do not want to go." Jesus said this to indicate the kind of death by which Peter would glorify God. Then he said to him, "Follow me!" (John 21:18-19, NIV)

Post-ascension

After the ascension of Christ, Peter immediately assumes a leadership role - it is Peter that drives the selection of a replacement apostle for Judas, in Acts 1:15-26. This leadership role is seemingly prefigured by Christ in Luke 22:32:

But I have prayed for you, Simon, that your faith may not fail. And when you have turned back, strengthen your brothers. (Luke 22:32, NIV)

Post-Pentecostal

16th century drawing showing Peter preaching to the multitudes[42]

After Pentecost, Peter, the simple Galilean fisherman, is transformed into a great preacher, healer, and fearless advocate for Jesus Christ. In fact, Peter is accorded the honor of being the first person to preach a sermon in the new church – a sermon that garners 3,000 new con-

---

42 Library of Congress LC-DIG-ppmsca-18668

verts! (Acts 2:14-41). Peter's activities in the Primitive Church are summarized below:

- In Acts 3, Peter heals a cripple near the Temple in Jerusalem, and again preaches a sermon at Solomon's Colonnade, which gathers at least 2,000 more converts (Acts 4:4)
- Peter and John are put in prison by the Sanhedrin (Acts 4:1-22). Peter, filled with the Holy Spirit, uses the occasion to preach the Gospel of Christ to the rulers of the Sanhedrin. One of the most important verses in all of Acts begins to explain why people gave credence to the early Christians:

  > When they saw the courage of Peter and John and realized that they were unschooled, ordinary men, they were astonished and they took note that these men had been with Jesus. (Acts 4:13, NIV)

- In Acts 5:1-11, Peter is the focus of the event which leads to the death of a husband and wife who lied about a contribution to the young church
- In Acts 5:15-16, people bring their sick to be healed by Peter and the other apostles
- In Acts 5:25-42, the apostles are arrested and brought before the Sanhedrin. Peter, the simple fisherman, once again uses the opportunity to lecture the learned Sanhedrin. After being flogged, the apostles are freed.
- In Acts 8:14-25, Peter and John are sent to Samaria to baptize by the laying on of hands. Peter then has a run-in with Simon Magus (Simon the Magician). Later church and apocryphal traditions indicate that the two will meet again in the future.
- In Acts 9:32-43, Peter raises a woman named Tabitha from the dead
- In Acts 10, Peter receives a vision, convincing him that the message of Christ is for Gentiles, too. In Acts 10:44-48, the ministry to the Gentiles blossoms.
- In Acts 11:1-18, Peter successfully defends the baptizing of Gentiles to the Jewish Christians in Jerusalem
- In Acts 12:1-9, Peter is arrested by King Herod Agrippa I, grandson of the Herod the Great, and thrown in prison. An angel rescues

Peter, perhaps because "the church was earnestly praying to God for him."

- In Acts 15:5-12, Peter plays a key role in convincing the Council of Jerusalem that Gentile converts should be allowed into the young church without restriction - "We believe it is through the grace of our Lord Jesus that we are saved, just as they are."
- Peter may have preached in Corinth (1 Cor 1:12)

Relationship of Peter with Paul

Peter and Paul[43]

The New Testament records that Peter and Paul, the two greatest apostles of the Early Church, did have some interaction with each other. Galatians 1:18, for example, records that Paul stayed with Peter in Jerusalem for a period of 15 days. Peter supports Paul's min-

---

istry to the Gentiles at the Jerusalem Council in Acts 15. This is further supported in Galatians 2:7-10, when Peter (a "pillar") is depicted as being an "apostle to the Jews", and supporting Paul's ministry to the Gentiles.

There were some disagreements between the two. In Galatians, 2:11-14 Paul describes an argument that he had with Peter in Antioch. In 2 Peter 3:15-16, Peter describes that Paul's letters are "hard to understand", but ascribes to them the same authority as the Jewish Scriptures:

> Bear in mind that our Lord's patience means salvation, just as our dear brother Paul also wrote you with the wisdom that God gave him. He writes the same way in all his letters, speaking in them of these matters. His letters contain some things that are hard to understand, which ignorant and unstable people distort, as they do the other Scriptures, to their own destruction. (2 Pet 3:15-16, NIV)

Keys to the Kingdom

The most controversial passages (in modern terms) in the New Testament regarding Peter are those describing Peter as the "rock" upon which Jesus will build his Church, and assigning him the "keys to the kingdom". The passages in question are below:

> And I tell you that you are Peter, and on this rock I will build my church, and the gates of Hades will not overcome it. I will give you the keys of the kingdom of heaven; whatever you bind on earth will be bound in heaven, and whatever you loose on earth will be loosed in heaven. (Mat 16:18-19, NIV)

These verses have been traditionally interpreted by the Roman Catholic Church as indicating that the Christian Church has received its authority from the legacy of Peter. The Roman Church also points to passages such as John 21:16, where Jesus says to Peter "Take care of my sheep", as further justification that Peter is the founder of the Christian Church.

Protestants have traditionally interpreted the "rock" and "keys" passages to indicate that the *faith* of Peter is the "rock upon which I will build my church", and that *faith* is the "keys to the kingdom." Protestants often view that Paul, not Peter, is the founder of the Christian Church as we know it today.

Church tradition (see below) also records that Peter was the first Bishop of Rome, and that all Catholic popes are spiritual descendents from Peter.

Mitigating against this Catholic view of Peter-as-the-first-Pope is the fact that nowhere in the Scriptures does it say that Peter preached in Rome. The closest is a cryptic remark at the end of 1 Peter:

> She who is in Babylon, chosen together with you, sends you her greetings, and so does my son Mark. (1 Peter 5:13, NIV)

Also of interest is the fact that the head of the early Jerusalem Church was James, brother of Jesus, not Peter, as noted in this passage from Eusebius:

> But Clement in the sixth book of his Hypotyposes writes thus: "For they say that Peter and James and John after the ascension of our Savior, as if also preferred by our Lord, strove not after honor, but chose James the Just bishop of Jerusalem." (*The Church History of Eusebius*, Translated By the Rev. Arthur Cushman Mcgiffert, Ph.D., Book 2, Chapter 1[44])

Church Tradition

Eusebius, quoting Papias of Hierapolis (c. 110 A.D.), records a tradition that the Gospel of Mark preserved the Gospel as preached by Peter:

> Mark having become the interpreter of Peter, wrote down accurately whatsoever he remembered...he accompanied Peter... (*The Church History of Eusebius*, Translated By the Rev. Arthur Cushman Mcgiffert, Ph.D., Book 3, Chapter 39[45])

---

44 *The Nicene and Post-Nicene Fathers Second Series, Volume 1*, by Philip Schaff, editor
45 *The Nicene and Post-Nicene Fathers Second Series, Volume 1*, by Philip Schaff, editor

Irenaeus (c. 180 A.D.) records a similar tradition, and mentions that Peter and Paul founded the Church in Rome:

> Matthew also issued a written Gospel among the Hebrews in their own dialect, while Peter and Paul were preaching at Rome, and laying the foundations of the Church. After their departure, Mark, the disciple and interpreter of Peter, did also hand down to us in writing what had been preached by Peter... (*Against Heresies*, Irenaeus, Translated by A. Cleveland Coxe, D.D., Book 3, Chapter 1[46])

Two letters in the New Testament are ascribed to Peter. 1 Peter has always been universally accepted as the writing of Peter, with some doubt cast on 2 Peter by some. Eusebius gives his opinion about Peter I and II:

> ONE epistle of Peter, that called the first, is acknowledged as genuine. And this the ancient elders used freely in their own writings as an undisputed work. But we have learned that his extant second Epistle does not belong to the canon; yet, as it has appeared profitable to many, it has been used with the other Scriptures. (*The Church History of Eusebius*, Translated By the Rev. Arthur Cushman Mcgiffert, Ph.D., Book 3, Chapter 3[47])

Eusebius also records the tradition that Peter preached in Rome, and fought against the heresy of Simon Magus (traditionally considered to be the founder of Gnosticism):

> For immediately, during the reign of Claudius, the all-good and gracious Providence, which watches over all things, led Peter, that strongest and greatest of the apostles, and the one who on account of his virtue was the speaker for all the others, to Rome against this great corrupter of life. He like a noble commander of God, clad in divine armor, carried the costly merchandise of the light of the understanding from the East to those who dwelt in the West, proclaiming the light itself, and the word which brings salvation to souls, and preaching the kingdom of heaven. (*The Church History of Eusebius*, Translated By the Rev. Arthur Cushman Mcgiffert, Ph.D., Book 2, Chapter 14[48])

---

46 *The Ante-Nicene Fathers Volume 1*, Edited by A. Roberts and J Donaldson
47 *Op Cit*
48 *The Nicene and Post-Nicene Fathers Second Series, Volume 1*, by Philip Schaff, editor

Eusebius records where Peter preached:

Peter appears to have preached in Pontus, Galatia, Bithynia, Cappadocia, and Asia to the Jews of the dispersion. And at last, having come to
Rome, he was crucified head-downwards; for he had requested that
he might suffer in this way. [Note: Pontus, Galatia, Bithynia, and Cappadocia are all located in modern northern Turkey] (*The Church History of Eusebius*, Translated By the Rev. Arthur Cushman Mcgiffert,
Ph.D., Book 3, Chapter 1[49])

Eusebius also records that Peter was put to death under Nero in Rome:

It is, therefore, recorded that Paul was beheaded in Rome itself, and
that Peter likewise was crucified under Nero. This account of Peter
and Paul is substantiated by the fact that their names are preserved in
the cemeteries of that place even to the present day. It is confirmed
likewise by Caius, a member of the Church, who arose under
Zephyrinus, bishop of Rome. He, in a published disputation with Pro-
clus, the leader of the Phrygian heresy, speaks as follows concerning
the places where the sacred corpses of the aforesaid apostles are laid:
"But I can show the trophies of the apostles. For if you will go to the
Vatican or to the Ostian way, you will find the trophies of those who
laid the foundations of this church." And that they both suffered martyrdom at the same time is stated by Dionysius, bishop of Corinth, in
his epistle to the Romans, in the following words: "You have thus by
such an admonition bound together the planting of Peter and of Paul
at Rome and Corinth. For both of them planted and likewise taught us
in our Corinth. And they taught together in like manner in Italy, and
suffered martyrdom at the same time." I have quoted these things in
order that the truth of the history might be still more confirmed. (*The
Church History of Eusebius*, Translated By the Rev. Arthur Cushman
Mcgiffert, Ph.D., Book 2, Chapter 25)[50]

According to Hippolytus, Peter was crucified by Nero in Rome:

Peter preached the Gospel in Pontus, and Galatia, and Cappadocia,
and Betania, and Italy, and Asia, and was afterwards crucified by Nero
in Rome with his head downward, as he had himself desired to suffer

---

49 *Ibid*
50 *Ibid*

in that manner. (*On the Twelve Apostles*, Hippolytus, Translated by A. Cleveland Coxe, D.D., Book 3, Chapter 30[51])

"The Apostle Peter being crucified upside down in Rome on orders of Nero, A.D. 69"[52]

Eusebius records a tradition from Clement of Alexandria regarding the martyrdom of the wife of Peter:

> They say, accordingly, that when the blessed Peter saw his own wife led out to die, he rejoiced because of her summons and her return home, and called to her very encouragingly and comfortingly, addressing her by name, and saying, "Oh thou, remember the Lord." Such was the marriage of the blessed, and their perfect disposition toward those dearest to them. (*The Church History of Eusebius*, Translated By the Rev. Arthur Cushman Mcgiffert, Ph.D.[53])

51 *The Ante-Nicene Fathers Volume 5*, Edited by A. Roberts and J Donaldson
52 *Martyrs Mirror*, by Thieleman J. van Braght, 1660
53 *The Nicene and Post-Nicene Fathers Second Series, Volume 1, by Philip Schaff, editor*

Church tradition records that Peter was buried in Rome on Vatican Hill, near the gardens of Nero. The first memorial over the grave was placed there in 160 A.D. A huge basilica was place there by Constantine in the 4th century. A series of excavations instituted by Pope Paul XII in 1940-51, and 1953-7 seems to have verified that the spire of the present St. Peter's Church in Rome is located about 300 feet above the underground grave of Peter.

Apocryphal

The *Acts Of The Holy Apostles Peter And Paul* discusses the ministry of Peter in Rome, where he converts the wife (Libia) of Nero to Christianity(!) The bulk of the apocryphal Acts describes the battle in Rome between Peter (and Paul) and Simon the Magician. The battle eventually plays out in front of Nero, and all three (Peter, Paul, Simon) end up dying. The death and burial of Peter is described thus:

> Then both Peter and Paul were led away from the presence of Nero. And Paul was beheaded on the Ostesian road. And Peter, having come to the cross, said: Since my Lord Jesus Christ, who came down from the heaven upon the earth, was raised upon the cross upright, and He has deigned to call to heaven me, who am of the earth, my cross ought to be fixed head downmost, so as to direct my feet towards heaven; for I am not worthy to be crucified like my Lord. Then, having reversed the cross, they nailed his feet up.

> And the consummation of the holy glorious Apostles Peter and Paul was on the 29th of the month of June -- (*Acts Of The Holy Apostles Peter And Paul*, Translated By Alexander Walker, Esq.[54])

A number of apocryphal writings are ascribed to Peter, including a Gospel, an Apocalypse, an Acts (of Peter and Paul), etc. Eusebius gives his opinion of these works:

> The so-called Acts of Peter, however, and the Gospel which bears his name, and the Preaching and the Apocalypse, as they are called, we know have not been universally accepted, because no ecclesiastical writer, ancient or modern, has made use of testimonies drawn from

---

54 *The Ante-Nicene Fathers Volume 8*, Edited by A. Roberts and J Donaldson

them. (*The Church History of Eusebius*, Translated By the Rev. Arthur Cushman Mcgiffert, Ph.D., Book 3, Chapter 3[55])

The second century Gospel of Peter describes the period of time after the death of Jesus, adding details to the story of Joseph of Arimathea, and the women at the tomb. Intriguingly, "Mary of Magdala" is described as a "disciple of the Lord".

Revelation of Peter

Possibly, one of the first known attempts by the Early Church Fathers to define a canon was in a fragmentary list (85 lines) dated to c. 200 A.D., named (after its 18th century discoverer, Lodovico Muratori) the Muratori Canon. The Muratori Canon is remarkably similar to our modern day New Testament, lacking only Philemon, Hebrews, James, I Peter, II Peter, and III John. The Muratori Canon also adds the Old Testament Apocryphal book "Wisdom of Solomon", as well as the "Revelation of Peter". Line 69 of the Muratori Canon indicates, in reference to the Revelation of Peter, "that some among us would not have [it] read in church." It was also quoted from by several of the Early Church Fathers, include Clement of Alexandria.

The Revelation of Peter was lost until 1886 when a French archaeological mission found fragments of it in Egypt. Most scholars view that the Revelation of Peter was written in the second century, thus, it could not have been written by Peter. However, it does seem to have some stylistic similarities with II Peter.

The extant fragments of the Revelation of Peter start out with the apostles asking Christ to:

> ...show us one of our brethren, the righteous who are gone forth out of the world, in order that we might see of what manner of form they are, and having taken courage, might also encourage the men who hear us. (*The Revelation of Peter*, Translated by Allan Menzies D. D.[56])

---

55 *The Nicene and Post-Nicene Fathers Second Series, Volume 1*, by Philip Schaff, editor

56 *The Ante-Nicene Fathers Volume 10*, Edited by A. Roberts and J Donaldson

After a visit from two angels, of whom Christ says "these are your brethren the righteous, whose forms ye desired to see", the apostles are shown the dwelling place of the righteous:

> And the Lord showed me a very great country outside of this world, exceeding bright with light, and the air there lighted with the rays of the sun, and the earth itself blooming with unfading flowers and full of spices and plants, fair-flowering and incorruptible and bearing blessed fruit...And the dwellers in that place were clad in the raiment of shining angels and their raiment was like unto their country; and angels hovered about them there. (*The Revelation of Peter*, Translated by Allan Menzies D. D.[57])

After this encounter, the tone of the Revelation of Peter turns decidedly darker, as the abode of the unrighteous is described in almost painful detail:

> And over against that place I saw another, squalid, and it was the place of punishment; and those who were punished there and the punishing angels had their raiment dark like the air of the place. And there were certain there hanging by the tongue: and these were the blasphemers of the way of righteousness; and under them lay fire, burning and punishing them. And there was a great lake, full of flaming mire, in which were certain men that pervert righteousness, and tormenting angels afflicted them. (*The Revelation of Peter*, Translated by Allan Menzies D. D.[58])

The fragment later ends in mid-description of hell, and in mid-sentence:

> And others again near them, women and men, burning and turning themselves and roasting: and these were they that leaving the way of God [end of fragment] (*The Revelation of Peter*, Translated by Allan Menzies D. D.[59])

---

57 *Ibid*
58 *Ibid*
59 *Ibid*

Chapter Nine – Philip

Medieval depiction of Philip[60]

Philip appears in all four lists of apostles in the New Testament, apparently linked with Bartholomew in the synoptic versions. This identification is enhanced in the Gospel of John. In John 1:43, Jesus finds Philip and tells him "Follow me". Philip (who is identified as being from Bethsaida in John 1:44) goes and tells his friend Nathanael (generally viewed as being Bartholomew, as in "Nathanael, son of Tolmai"):

> Philip found Nathanael and told him, "We have found the one Moses wrote about in the Law, and about whom the prophets also wrote--Jesus of Nazareth, the son of Joseph." (John 1:45, NIV)

---

60 Library of Congress LC-DIG-ppmsca-18692

It is possible that Philip acted in the role of quartermaster or provisioner for Jesus and the apostles, for when Jesus is about to perform his miracle of feeding the 5,000, he says:

> When Jesus looked up and saw a great crowd coming toward him, he said to Philip, "Where shall we buy bread for these people to eat?" He asked this only to test him, for he already had in mind what he was going to do. Philip answered him, "Eight months' wages would not buy enough bread for each one to have a bite!" (John 6:5-7, NIV)

Jesus preaches to the 5,000 (Photo by Robert Jones)[61]

Philip also appears in John when a group of Greeks ask him to meet Jesus. After collecting Andrew, the two inform Jesus that he has visitors. (John 12:20-22)

---

61 From a stained glass window at Mars Hill Presbyterian Church, Acworth, GA

At the Last Supper, in John 14:6-9, Philip asks Jesus to "show us the Father", and Jesus replies "Anyone who has seen me has seen the Father."

Church Tradition

According to Hippolytus, Philip preached and was executed in what today is eastern Turkey:

> Philip preached in Phrygia, and was crucified in Hierapolis with his head downward in the time of Domitian, and was buried there. (*On the Twelve Apostles*, Hippolytus, Translated by A. Cleveland Coxe, D.D.[62])

According to Eusebius (quoting Clement of Alexandria) Philip was married, and had daughters:

> For Peter and Philip begat children; and Philip also gave his daughters in marriage... (*The Church History of Eusebius*, Translated By the Rev. Arthur Cushman Mcgiffert, Ph.D., Book 3, Chapter 30[63])

Eusebius, quoting Polycrates, discusses the death of Philip and his daughters:

> For in Asia also great lights have fallen asleep, which shall rise again on the last day, at the coming of the Lord, when he shall come with glory from heaven and shall seek out all the saints. Among these are Philip, one of the twelve apostles, who sleeps in Hierapolis, and his two aged virgin daughters, and another daughter who lived in the Holy Spirit and now rests at Ephesus... (*The Church History of Eusebius*, Translated By the Rev. Arthur Cushman Mcgiffert, Ph.D., Book 3, Chapter 31[64])

Referencing Papias, Eusebius records a tradition that one of Philip's daughters rose from the dead (it is unclear in the text as to whether Philip did the raising):

---

62 *The Ante-Nicene Fathers Volume 5*, Edited by A. Roberts and J Donaldson
63 *The Nicene and Post-Nicene Fathers Second Series, Volume 1*, by Philip Schaff, editor
64 *Ibid*

That Philip the apostle dwelt at Hierapolis with his daughters has been already stated. But it must be noted here that Papias, their contemporary, says that he heard a wonderful tale from the daughters of Philip. For he relates that in his time one rose from the dead. (*The Church History of Eusebius*, Translated By the Rev. Arthur Cushman Mcgiffert, Ph.D., Book 3, Chapter 39[65])

It should be noted, though, that there seems to be at least some confusion in the works of the ancients regarding the daughters of Philip the Apostle, and Philip the Deacon (Acts 6:5, Acts 21:8-9).

Apocryphal

The apocryphal *Acts Of The Journeyings Of Philip The Apostle* has Philip preaching in the "cities and regions of Lydia and Asia". After converting the wife of the Roman proconsul, Philip is captured by the irate husband and hung upside down:

And he ordered Philip to be hanged, and his ankles to be pierced, and to bring also iron hooks, and his heels also to be driven through, and to be hanged head downwards, opposite the temple on a certain tree... (*Acts Of The Journeyings Of Philip The Apostle*, Translated By Alexander Walker, Esq.[66])

An angry Philip places a curse on his captors, and 7,000 men (including the proconsul) are swept into an abyss. Jesus appears and reprimands Philip for rendering evil for evil. Philip's punishment is that he will not be able to enter paradise for 40 days after he dies. After Philip "gives up the ghost":

...the plant of the vine sprouted up where the blood of the holy Philip had dropped...And they built the church in that place... (*Acts Of The Journeyings Of Philip The Apostle*, Translated By Alexander Walker, Esq.[67])

In the second part of the same Acts, Philip preaches in Athens in front of 300 philosophers, and eventually ends up in a battle with the Jewish High Priest Ananias (from Jerusalem). Although Philip performs many miracles, Ananias refuses to believe in Christ. Philip buries him,

---

65 *Ibid*
66 *The Ante-Nicene Fathers Volume 8*, Edited by A. Roberts and J Donaldson
67 *Ibid*

in stages, up to his knees, navel, and neck – and finally consigns him to the Abyss (Hades). The Acts end with:

> And Philip abode in Athens two years; and having founded a church, appointed a bishop and a presbyter, and so went away to Parthia [probably near modern day Tehran], preaching Christ. To whom be glory for ever. Amen. (*Acts Of The Journeyings Of Philip The Apostle,* Translated By Alexander Walker, Esq.[68])

---

68 *Ibid*

Chapter Ten - Simon the Zealot

Simon the Zealot is mentioned in all four lists of apostles in the New Testament – and no other information is given about him whatsoever. Traditionally, Simon is thought to have been a member of the Jewish Zealot party, a group of nationalists that eventually revolted (disastrously) against the Romans in 66 A.D. However, the name could also be translated "the zealous one".

Church Tradition

According to Hippolytus, Simon the Zealot was the second Bishop of Jerusalem:

> Simon the Zealot, the son of Clopas, who is also called Jude, became bishop of Jerusalem after James the Just, and fell asleep and was buried there at the age of 120 years. (*On the Twelve Apostles*, Hippolytus, Translated by A. Cleveland Coxe, D.D.[69])

Eusebius identifies that "Symeon, the son of Clopas," was the second Bishop of Jerusalem, but he does not specifically connect this figure with Simon the Zealot.

The apocryphal *Passion of Simon and Jude* places Simon in Persia.

---

69 *The Ante-Nicene Fathers Volume 5*, Edited by A. Roberts and J Donaldson

Chapter Eleven - Thaddaeus/Judas son of James

Matthew and Mark refer to an apostle named Thaddaeus in their apostolic list. Luke (in both lists) refers to a "Judas, son of James". Generally, scholars feel these are one and the same. Some manuscripts mention yet a third name – Lebbaeus, as shown in this verse from the King James Version:

> Philip, and Bartholomew; Thomas, and Matthew the publican; James the son of Alphaeus, and **Lebbaeus, whose surname was Thaddaeus**... (Matthew 10:3, KJV; emphasis added)

Thaddaeus/Judas possibly shows up in John, asking the following question:

> Then Judas (not Judas Iscariot) said, "But, Lord, why do you intend to show yourself to us and not to the world?" Jesus replied, "If anyone loves me, he will obey my teaching. My Father will love him, and we will come to him and make our home with him." (John 14:22-23, NIV)

Some scholars identify Thaddaeus/Judas as the author of Jude, but most scholars view the author of Jude as being the brother of Jesus and James (the Just).

Church Tradition

Hippolytus records:

> Jude, who is also called Lebbaeus, preached to the people of Edessa, and to all Mesopotamia, and fell asleep at Berytus, and was buried there. (*On the Twelve Apostles*, Hippolytus, Translated by A. Cleveland Coxe, D.D.[70])

Eusebius reports the contents of a Syriac manuscript that reports that Thaddaeus was sent by Thomas to Edessa, to heal and preach:

> After the ascension of Jesus, Judas, who was also called Thomas, sent to him Thaddeus, an apostle, one of the Seventy. When he was come he lodged with Tobias, the son of Tobias. When the report of him got abroad, it was told Abgarus that an apostle of Jesus was come, as he

---

70 *The Ante-Nicene Fathers Volume 5*, Edited by A. Roberts and J Donaldson

had written him. Thaddeus began then in the power of God to heal every disease and infirmity...The same Thaddeus cured also many other inhabitants of the city, and did wonders and marvelous works, and preached the word of God. (*The Church History of Eusebius*, Translated By the Rev. Arthur Cushman Mcgiffert, Ph.D., Book 1, Chapter 13[71])

Apocryphal

The apocryphal *Acts Of The Holy Apostle Thaddaeus - One Of The Twelve* tells us that Thaddaeus was from the city of Edessa, and was a follower of John the Baptist:

> LEBBAEUS, who also is Thaddaeus, was of the city of Edessa — and it is the metropolis of Osroene, in the interior of the Armenosyrians — an Hebrew by race, accomplished and most learned in the divine writings. He came to Jerusalem to worship in the days of John the Baptist; and having heard his preaching and seen his angelic life, he was baptized, and his name was called Thaddaeus. And having seen the appearing of Christ, and His teaching, and His wonderful works, he followed Him, and became His disciple; and He chose him as one of the twelve, the tenth apostle according to the Evangelists Matthew and Mark. (*Acts Of The Holy Apostle Thaddaeus - One Of The Twelve*, Translated By Alexander Walker, Esq.[72])

In the Acts, the Governor of Edessa, Abgarus, contracts an incurable disease. He sends a letter to Jesus (!), asking for help. In the course of the reply, Jesus promises to send Thaddeus to Edessa. The passage is interesting, because it seems to foreshadow the Shroud of Turin:

> And Ananias [a courier], having gone and given the letter, was carefully looking at Christ, but was unable to fix Him in his mind. And He knew as knowing the heart, and asked to wash Himself; and a towel was given Him; and when He had washed Himself, He wiped His face with it. And His image having been imprinted upon the linen, He gave it to Ananias, saying: Give this, and take back this message, to him that sent thee: Peace to thee and thy city! For because of this I am come, to suffer for the world, and to rise again, and to raise up the forefathers. And after I have been taken up into the heavens I shall send thee my disciple Thaddaeus, who shall enlighten thee, and guide

---

71 *The Nicene and Post-Nicene Fathers Second Series, Volume 1*, by Philip Schaff, editor
72 *The Ante-Nicene Fathers Volume 8*, Edited by A. Roberts and J Donaldson

thee into all the truth, both thee and thy city. (*Acts Of The Holy Apostle Thaddaeus - One Of The Twelve*, Translated By Alexander Walker, Esq.[73])

Thaddaeus eventually baptizes Abgarus, and establishes churches in Edessa and throughout Syria. Finally, the Acts report that Thaddaeus died in Berytus in Phoencia:

> And Thaddaeus along with Abgarus destroyed idol-temples and built churches; ordained as bishop one of his disciples, and presbyters, and deacons, and gave them the rule of the psalmody and the holy liturgy. And having left them, he went to the city of Amis, great metropolis of the Mesechaldeans and Syrians, that is, of Mesopotamia-Syria, beside the river Tigris.
>
> Having therefore remained with them for five years, he built a church; and having appointed as bishop one of his disciples, and presbyters, and deacons, and prayed for them, he went away, going round the cities of Syria, and teaching, and healing all the sick; whence he brought many cities and countries to Christ through His teaching. Teaching, therefore, and evangelizing along with the disciples, and healing the sick, he went to Berytus, a city of Phoenicia by the sea; and there, having taught and enlightened many, he fell asleep on the twenty-first of the month of August. And the disciples having come together, buried him with great honor; and many sick were healed, and they gave glory to the Father, and the Son, and the Holy Spirit, for ever and ever. Amen. (*Acts Of The Holy Apostle Thaddaeus - One Of The Twelve*, Translated By Alexander Walker, Esq.[74])

This Acts may have slightly more credibility than some others, as many of the story elements are quoted by Eusebius in his Church History (Abgarus writing to Jesus, Jesus writing back (!), Thaddaeus journeying to Edessa to heal, etc.)

> THE divinity of our Lord and Savior Jesus Christ being noised abroad among all men on account of his wonder-working power, he attracted countless numbers from foreign countries lying far away from Judea, who had the opening of being cured of their diseases and of all kinds of sufferings. For instance the King Abgarus, who ruled with great glory the nations beyond the Euphrates, being afflicted with a terrible disease which it was beyond the power of human skill to cure, when

---

73 *Ibid*
74 *Ibid*

he heard of the name of Jesus, and of his miracles, which were attested by all with one accord sent a message to him by a courier and begged him to heal his disease. But he did not at that time comply with his request; yet he deemed him worthy of a personal letter in which he said that he would send one of his disciples to cure his disease, and at the same time promised salvation to himself and all his house. Not long afterward his promise was fulfilled. For after his resurrection from the dead and his ascent into heaven, Thomas, one of the twelve apostles, under divine impulse sent Thaddeus, who was also numbered among the seventy disciples of Christ, to Edessa, as a preacher and evangelist of the teaching of Christ. And all that our Savior had promised received through him its fulfillment. You have written evidence of these things taken from the archives of Edessa, which was at that time a royal city. For in the public registers there, which contain accounts of ancient times and the acts of Abgarus, these things have been found preserved down to the present time. (*The Church History of Eusebius*, Translated By the Rev. Arthur Cushman Mcgiffert, Ph.D., Book 1, Chapter 13[75])

Eusebius then records the letters exchanged between Abgarus and Jesus. Here is the supposed reply from Jesus to Abgarus:

THE ANSWER OF JESUS TO THE RULER ABGARUS BY THE COURIER ANANIAS.
Blessed art thou who hast believed in me without having seen me. For it is written concerning me, that they who have seen me will not believe in me, and that they who have not seen me will believe and be saved. But in regard to what thou hast written me, that I should come to thee, it is necessary for me to fulfill all things here for which I have been sent, and after I have fulfilled them thus to be taken up again to him that sent me. But after I have been taken up I will send to thee one of my disciples, that he may heal thy disease and give life to thee and thine. (*The Church History of Eusebius*, Translated By the Rev. Arthur Cushman Mcgiffert, Ph.D., Book 1, Chapter 13[76])

---

75 *The Nicene and Post-Nicene Fathers Second Series, Volume 1,* by Philip Schaff, editor
76 *Ibid*

Chapter Twelve – Thomas

Thomas appears in all four New Testament lists of Apostles. In the Gospel of John, Thomas's name is listed as "Thomas (called Didymus)". *Didymus* is Greek for "twin" or "double". Because the name Thomas is linked with Matthew in the three apostolic lists in the Synoptic Gospels (see, for example, Matt 10:3), some scholars have postulated that Thomas and Matthew were twin brothers.

Thomas appears several times in interesting roles in the Gospel of John. In the 11th chapter of John, Thomas makes the following curious statement when Jesus suggests that the disciples visit the dead Lazarus:

> Then Thomas (called Didymus) said to the rest of the disciples, "Let us also go, that we may die with him." (John 11:16, NIV)

Thomas also has the distinction of asking the question that prompts one of the most famous answers in the Bible:

> Thomas said to him, "Lord, we don't know where you are going, so how can we know the way?" Jesus answered, "I am the way and the truth and the life. No one comes to the Father except through me." (John 14:5-6, NIV)

However, Thomas is most famous for his doubting that Jesus had resurrected from the dead, earning the sobriquet "Doubting Thomas". The incident is described in John 20:24-29, and quotes Thomas as saying "Unless I see the nail marks in his hands and put my finger where the nails were, and put my hand into his side, I will not believe it."

Finally, Thomas is present on the Sea of Galilea when Jesus causes a miraculous catch of fish, and prepares breakfast for the apostles on the beach.

Church Tradition

Hippolytus records that Thomas was an active missionary, and that he met his fate in India:

And Thomas preached to the Parthians, Medes, Persians, Hyrcanians, Bactrians, and Margians, and was thrust through in the four members of his body with a pine spear at Calamene, the city of India, and was buried there. (*On the Twelve Apostles*, Hippolytus, Translated by A. Cleveland Coxe, D.D.[77])

"Thomas, tortured by the natives in Calamina, thrown into an oven, and stuck through with spears, AD 70"[78]

Eusebius in his Church History records that Thomas sent other disciples out on missionary journeys:

Thomas, one of the twelve apostles, under divine impulse sent Thaddeus, who was also numbered among the seventy disciples of Christ, to Edessa, as a preacher and evangelist of the teaching of Christ. (*The Church History of Eusebius*, Translated By the Rev. Arthur Cushman Mcgiffert, Ph.D., Book 1, Chapter 13[79])

---

77 *The Ante-Nicene Fathers Volume 5*, Edited by A. Roberts and J Donaldson

78 *Martyrs Mirror*, Thieleman J. van Braght, 1660

79 *The Nicene and Post-Nicene Fathers Second Series, Volume 1*, by Philip Schaff, editor

Eusebius records that Thomas preached in Parthia (near modern-day Tehran):

> Parthia, according to tradition, was allotted to Thomas as his field of labor... (*The Church History of Eusebius*, Translated By the Rev. Arthur Cushman Mcgiffert, Ph.D., Book 3, Chapter 1[80])

Apocryphal

In the *Acts Of The Holy Apostle Thomas*, a reluctant Thomas is assigned missionary duty in India:

> AT that time we the apostles were all in Jerusalem...and we portioned out the regions of the world, in order that each one of us might go into the region that fell to him, and to the nation to which the Lord sent him. By lot, then, India fell to Judas Thomas, also called Didymus. And he did not wish to go, saying that he was not able to go on account of the weakness of the flesh; and how can I, being an Hebrew man, go among the Indians to proclaim the truth? And while he was thus reasoning and speaking, the Savior appeared to him through the night, and said to him: Fear not, Thomas; go away to India, and proclaim the word; for my grace shall be with thee. (*Acts Of The Holy Apostle Thomas*, Translated By Alexander Walker, Esq.[81])

In the same apocryphal acts, Jesus appears as the brother of Thomas:

> And he saw the Lord Jesus talking with the bride, and having the appearance of Judas Thomas, who shortly before had blessed them, and gone out from them; and he says to him: "Didst thou not go out before them all? And how art thou found here?" And the Lord said to him: "I am not Judas, who also is Thomas; I am his brother."
>
> "...I know that thou art the twin-brother of Christ..." (*Acts Of The Holy Apostle Thomas*, Translated By Alexander Walker, Esq.[82])

Some people believe that this tradition is preserved in Da Vinci's *Last Supper* – note the apostle on the far left who looks very much like Jesus.

---

80 *Ibid*
81 *The Ante-Nicene Fathers Volume 8*, Edited by A. Roberts and J Donaldson
82 *Ibid*

After an active career as a preacher and healer, Thomas is put to death by order of a King Misdeus, on the charge of heresy. In this account, Thomas is executed by spear:

> And when he had prayed, he said to the soldiers: Come and finish the work of him that sent you. And the four struck him at once, and killed him. And all the brethren wept, and wrapped him up in beautiful shawls, and many linen cloths, and laid him in the tomb in which of old the kings used to be buried. (*Acts Of The Holy Apostle Thomas*, Translated By Alexander Walker, Esq.[83])

Later, King Misdeus believes that the bones of the apostle may be able to heal his daughter, who is possessed by a demon. When he goes to the tomb "he did not find the bones (for one of the brethren had taken them, and carried them into the regions of the West)."

Two Gospels have appeared in the name of Thomas. One is an infancy Gospel, purporting to discuss the "great things which our Lord Jesus Christ did in His childhood". The second is a Gnostic Gospel, purporting to tell secret sayings of Jesus recorded by Thomas.

---

83 *Ibid*

Part Two – After the Twelve

Chapter Thirteen - Andronicus and Junias

Andronicus and Junias are mentioned in one verse in Romans, and may have been apostles. The verse in question is Romans 16:7:

> Greet Andronicus and Junias, my relatives who have been in prison with me. They are outstanding among the apostles, and they were in Christ before I was." (Romans 16:7, NIV)

This seemingly innocent passage has generated some controversy over the years for two reasons. First, does "outstanding among the apostles" mean that they were "outstanding apostles", or simply that they were well known among the apostles? If "outstanding apostles" is the correct interpretation, it leads into the second controversy - Junias is the feminine form of a Greek name. If this is the correct interpretation, then we have a female apostle.

The Revised Standard Version muddies the waters by stating, "they are men of note among the apostles". However, Junias (*Iounias*) is clearly of the feminine form, as Thayer's Greek Definitions states:

> "1) a Christian woman at Rome, mentioned by Paul as one of his kinsfolk and fellow prisoners
> Part of Speech: noun proper feminine"

St. John Chrysostom (c. 345-407), Patriarch of Constantinople, referred to Junias as a female apostle in one of his sermons:

> And indeed to be apostles at all is a great thing. But to be even amongst these of note, just consider what a great encomium this is! But they were of note owing to their works, to their achievements. Oh! how great is the devotion of this woman, that she should be even counted worthy of the appellation of apostle! (Homily 31, *Homilies of St. John Chrysostom Archbishop of Constantinople on the Epistle of St. Paul the Apostle to the Romans,* Translated By Rev. J. R. Morris, M.A. and Rev. W. H. Simcox[84])

---

84 *The Nicene and Post-Nicene Fathers First Series, Volume 11,* by Philip Schaff, editor

So, there is some evidence that there was a female post-twelve apostle.

Regarding other aspects of the passage, Paul tells us:

- They are Paul's relatives
- They spent time in prison with him (assumedly in Rome)
- They were "in Christ" before Paul was

Some commentators view that Andronicus and Junias were a married couple, similar to Priscilla and Aquila.

Chapter Fourteen - Barnabas

Barnabas was a "Levite from Cyprus". We are told in Acts 4 that his name means "Son of Encouragement":

> Joseph, a Levite from Cyprus, whom the apostles called Barnabas (which means Son of Encouragement), sold a field he owned and brought the money and put it at the apostles' feet." (Acts 4:36-37, NIV)

Barnabas was an early mentor and sponsor of Paul, introducing him to the apostles in Jerusalem after Paul's conversion. Barnabas and Paul spent at least a year in Antioch (Syria), where the term "Christian" was first used. Later, Barnabas would accompany Paul on his first missionary journey, and seems to have been in charge during at least some parts of the journey. He must have been a large man, because in Lystra, the people mistook him for Zeus!

Barnabas and Paul were key participants in the Jerusalem Council described in Acts 15. They represented the view that the Gentiles did not have to be circumcised in order to be saved.

Later, Barnabas and Paul parted company in a dispute over John Mark, the cousin of Barnabas. John Mark had "deserted them in Pamphylia" according to Paul, and Paul did not want him to accompany them on his second missionary journey. It was a "sharp disagreement", and Paul chose Silas instead of Barnabas to go with him on his second missionary journey.

Barnabas is identified as an apostle in Acts 14:14.

Reference	Verse(s)
"Joseph, a Levite from Cyprus, whom the apostles called Barnabas…"	Acts 4:36-37
"But Barnabas took him [Paul] and brought him to the apostles…"	Acts 9:27
Barnabas in Antioch	Acts 11:22-30
Barnabas, Saul and John Mark	Acts 12:25
Barnabas and Paul, led by the Holy Spirit, be-	Acts 13:1-13

Reference	Verse(s)
gin their missionary journey	
Barnabas and Paul make both Jewish and Gentile converts	Acts 13:42-52
Barnabas and Paul narrowly escape stoning in Iconium	Acts 14:1-7
Barnabas is mistaken for Zeus!	Acts 14:12
Barnabas and Paul appoint elders in Lystra, Iconium and Antioch	Acts 14:21-28
"But when the apostles Barnabas and Paul heard of this..."	Acts 14:14
Barnabas and Paul make their case at the Jerusalem Council	Acts 15:1-12
Barnabas and Paul are sent back to Antioch with the results of the Jerusalem Council	Acts 15:22-25
The great dispute between Barnabas and Paul	Acts 15:35-41
"Or is it only I and Barnabas who must work for a living?"	1 Cor. 9:6
Barnabas led astray	Gal 2:13
"Mark, the cousin of Barnabas..."	Col 4:10

Church tradition

According to Eusebius, Barnabas was "one of the seventy" original disciples of Jesus:

> The names of the apostles of our Savior are known to every one from the Gospels. But there exists no catalogue of the seventy disciples. Barnabas, indeed, is said to have been one of them, of whom the Acts of the apostles makes mention in various places, and especially Paul in his Epistle to the Galatians. (*The Church History of Eusebius*, Translated By the Rev. Arthur Cushman Mcgiffert, Ph.D., Book 1, Chapter 12[85])

Epistle of Barnabas

Barnabas may have been the author of a book that "almost" made the New Testament. The *Epistle of Barnabas* was deemed scripture by Clement of Alexandria, Origen, and Jerome. Eusebius branded it "rejected" in his *Ecclesiastical History*, but not heretical. It is also pos-

---

85 *The Nicene and Post-Nicene Fathers Second Series, Volume 1*, by Philip Schaff, editor

sibly written by a follower of Barnabas, perhaps at the end of the first century/beginning of the second.

The letter itself contains no authorship attribution. As to the date, we can say for sure that it was written after 70 A.D., because the fall of Jerusalem was recorded:

> Moreover, I will also tell you concerning the temple, how the wretched [Jews], wandering in error, trusted not in God Himself, but in the temple, as being the house of God...**For through their going to war, it was destroyed by their enemies**; and now: they, as the servants of their enemies, shall rebuild it. (*The Apostolic Fathers with Justin Martyr And Irenaeus*, Translated By A. Cleveland Coxe, D.D.[86])

The first major theme of the Epistle of Barnabas concerns demonstrating that the messianic prophesies in the Old Testament did indeed refer to Jesus. Christ is prefigured in the Jewish scapegoat, in Abraham, in Moses, and in Joshua (curiously, though, not Melchizedek). Both the cross and Christian baptism are prefigured in the Old Testament. Regarding the meaning of Christian baptism:

> ...we indeed descend into the water full of sins and defilement, but come up, bearing fruit in our heart, having the fear [of God] and trust in Jesus in our spirit... (*The Apostolic Fathers with Justin Martyr And Irenaeus*, Translated By A. Cleveland Coxe, D.D.[87])

The second major theme of the Letter of Barnabas is the path to salvation:

> As far as was possible, and could be done with perspicuity, I cherish the hope that, according to my desire, I have omitted none of those things at present [demanding consideration], which bear upon your salvation.

> There are two ways of doctrine and authority, the one of light, and the other of darkness. But there is a great difference between these two ways. For over one are stationed the light-bringing angels of God, but over the other the angels of Satan. And He indeed (i.e., God) is Lord for ever and ever, but he (i.e., Satan) is prince of the time of iniquity.

---

86 *The Ante-Nicene Fathers Volume 1*, Edited By A. Roberts And J Donaldson
87 *Ibid*

It is well, therefore, that he who has learned the judgments of the Lord, as many as have been written, should walk in them. For he who keepeth these shall be glorified in the kingdom of God; but he who chooseth other things shall be destroyed with his works. On this account there will be a resurrection, on this account a retribution...For the day is at hand on which all things shall perish with the evil [one]. The Lord is near, and His reward. (*The Apostolic Fathers with Justin Martyr And Irenaeus*, Translated By A. Cleveland Coxe, D.D.[88])

After the canon was fixed in the fourth century, the Letter of Barnabas faded into obscurity.

Apocryphal

The *Acts of Barnabas: The Journeyings and Martyrdom of St. Barnabas the Apostle*, purportedly written by John Mark, describes a missionary journey by Barnabas and Mark after the break with Paul (Acts 15:35-41). According to this apocryphal Acts, Barnabas used the Gospel of Matthew in his teachings:

And Barnabas had received documents from Matthew, a book of the word of God, and a narrative of miracles and doctrines. This Barnabas laid upon the sick in each place that we came to, and it immediately made a cure of their sufferings. (*Acts of Barnabas: The Journeyings and Martyrdom of St. Barnabas the Apostle*, Translated By Alexander Walker, Esq.[89])

According to this Acts, Barnabas met his fate in Salamis (Cyprus) at the hands of "Barjesus" (assumedly the same Bar-Jesus mentioned in Acts 13:6-12):

And Barjesus, having arrived after two days, after not a few Jews had been instructed, was enraged, and brought together all the multitude of the Jews...the Jews...took Barnabas by night, and bound him with a rope by the neck; and having dragged him to the hippodrome from the synagogue, and having gone out of the city, standing round him, they burned him with fire, so that even his bones became dust. (*Acts of Barnabas: The Journeyings and Martyrdom of St. Barnabas the Apostle*, Translated By Alexander Walker, Esq.[90])

---

88 *Ibid*
89 *The Ante-Nicene Fathers Volume 8*, Edited by A. Roberts and J Donaldson
90 *Ibid*

Chapter Fifteen - James the Just

James, brother of Jesus, plays almost no role in the earthly ministry of Jesus. However, after the Ascension of Jesus, James is present at the earliest meetings of the nascent church, and eventually assumes a leadership position in the Jerusalem Church, as can be seen by his seeming "first among equal" role at the Jerusalem Council (Acts 15). He is seemingly identified as an apostle in Galatians 1:19:

> I saw none of the other apostles—only James, the Lord's brother. (Galatians 1:19, NIV)

Church tradition says that James, brother of Jesus, wrote the book of James in the New Testament, although the author assignation in James 1:1 is ambiguous. (One of several places in the New Testament where it is difficult to ascertain which "James" is being referenced! – see also 1 Cor 15:7).

Reference	Verse(s)
"Isn't this the carpenter's son? Isn't his mother's name Mary, and aren't his brothers James, Joseph, Simon and Judas?"	Mat 13:55, Mark 6:3
The brothers of Jesus join the apostles after the Ascension of Jesus	Acts 1:14
Peter says, "Tell James and the brothers about this" after being released from prison by and angel	Acts 12:17
James makes the final decision at the Jerusalem Council	Acts 15:13
"The next day Paul and the rest of us went to see James, and all the elders were present."	Acts 21:18
James as an apostle	Gal 1:19
"James, Peter and John, those reputed to be pillars, gave me and Barnabas the right hand of fellowship..." [Note: This could also refer to James, son of Zebedee]	Gal 2:9
"Before certain men came from James..."	Gal 2:12

Church Tradition

James is mentioned by Josephus in his massive work *Jewish Antiquities*. We are told that James was sentenced by the Sanhedrin to be stoned:

> But this younger Ananus, who, as we have told you already, took the high priesthood, was a bold man in his temper, and very insolent; he was also of the sect of the Sadducees, who are very rigid in judging offenders, above all the rest of the Jews, as we have already observed; when, therefore, Ananus was of this disposition, he thought he had now a proper opportunity [to exercise his authority]. Festus was now dead, and Albinus was but upon the road; so he assembled the sanhedrim of judges, and brought before them the brother of Jesus, who was called Christ, whose name was James, and some others, [or, some of his companions]; and when he had formed an accusation against them as breakers of the law, he delivered them to be stoned: (*Jewish Antiquities*, Josephus, 20.9.1[91])

Eusebius is quite verbose regarding James, and adds details such as:

*   He was surnamed "the Just" on account of his virtue
*   He was the first bishop of Jerusalem
*   He was "thrown from the pinnacle of the Temple" and clubbed to death, because the Sanhedrin was frustrated by the escape of Paul to Rome
*   Eusebius argues that James was the "son of Joseph" (but not necessarily the son of Mary)
*   Quoting Hegesippus, it appears that James was a Nazorite from birth
*   The siege of Jerusalem by Titus was a direct result of the murder of the righteous James. Assuming that the siege happened soon after the death of James, his death would have been c. 66 A.D.

> Then James, whom the ancients surnamed the Just on account of the excellence of his virtue, is recorded to have been the first to be made bishop of the church of Jerusalem. This James was called the brother of the Lord because he was known as a son of Joseph, and Joseph was supposed to be the father of Christ, because the Virgin, being betrothed to him, "was found with child by the Holy Ghost before they

91 *The Works of Josephus*, Translated by William Whitson

came together," as the account of the holy Gospels shows. But Clement in the sixth book of his Hypotyposes writes thus: "For they say that Peter and James and John after the ascension of our Savior, as if also preferred by our Lord, strove not after honor, but chose James the Just bishop of Jerusalem." But the same writer, in the seventh book of the same work, relates also the following things concerning him: "The Lord after his resurrection imparted knowledge to James the Just and to John and Peter, and they imparted it to the rest of the apostles, and the rest of the apostles to the seventy, of whom Barnabas was one. But there were two Jameses: one called the Just, who was thrown from the pinnacle of the temple and was beaten to death with a club by a fuller, and another who was beheaded." Paul also makes mention of the same James the Just, where he writes, "Other of the apostles saw I none, save James the Lord's brother." (Eusebius, Book 2, Chapter 1)

"BUT after Paul, in consequence of his appeal to Caesar, had been sent to Rome by Festus, the Jews, being frustrated in their hope of entrapping him by the snares which they had laid for him, turned against James, the brother of the Lord, to whom the episcopal seat at Jerusalem had been entrusted by the apostles. The following daring measures were undertaken by them against him. Leading him into their midst they demanded of him that he should renounce faith in Christ in the presence of all the people.

But, contrary to the opinion of all, with a clear voice, and with greater boldness than they had anticipated, he spoke out before the whole multitude and confessed that our Savior and Lord Jesus is the Son of God. But they were unable to bear longer the testimony of the man who, on account of the excellence of ascetic virtue and of piety which he exhibited in his life, was esteemed by all as the most just of men, and consequently they slew him. Opportunity for this deed of violence was furnished by the prevailing anarchy, which was caused by the fact that Festus had died just at this time in Judea, and that the province was thus without a governor and head.

The manner of James' death has been already indicated by the above-quoted words of Clement, who records that he was thrown from the pinnacle of the temple, and was beaten to death with a club. But Hegesippus, who lived immediately after the apostles, gives the most accurate account in the fifth book of his Memoirs. He writes as follows: "James, the brother of the Lord, succeeded to the government of the Church in conjunction with the apostles. He has been called the Just by all from the time of our Savior to the present day; for there were many that bore the name of James. He was holy from his mother's womb; and he drank no wine nor strong drink, nor did he eat flesh. No razor came upon his head; he did not anoint himself with oil, and he did not use the bath. He alone was permitted to enter into the holy place; for he wore not woolen but linen garments. And he was in the habit of entering alone into the temple, and was frequently found upon his knees begging forgiveness for the people, so that his knees became hard like those of a camel, in consequence of his constantly bending them in his worship of God, and asking forgiveness for the people. Because of his exceeding great justice he was called the Just, and Oblias, which signifies in Greek, Bulwark of the people' and 'Justice,' in accordance with what the prophets declare concerning him....

So they went up and threw down the just man, and said to each other, 'Let us stone James the Just.' And they began to stone him, for he was not killed by the fall; but he turned and knelt down and said, 'I entreat thee, Lord God our Father, forgive them, for they know not what they do.' And while they were thus stoning him one of the priests of the sons of Rechab, the son of the Rechabites, who are mentioned by Jeremiah the prophet, cried out, saying, 'Cease, what do ye? The just one prayeth for you. And one of them, who was a fuller, took the club with which he beat out clothes and struck the just man on the head. And thus he suffered martyrdom. And they buried him on the spot, by the temple, and his monument still remains by the temple. He became a true witness, both to Jews and Greeks, that Jesus is the Christ. And immediately Vespasian besieged them."

These things are related at length by Hegesippus, who is in agreement with Clement. James was so admirable a man and so celebrated among all for his justice, that the more sensible even of the Jews were of the opinion that this was the cause of the siege of Jerusalem, which happened to them immediately after his martyrdom for no other reason than their daring act against him". (*The Church History of Eusebius*, Translated By the Rev. Arthur Cushman Mcgiffert, Ph.D., Book 2, Chapter 23[92])

The James Ossuary

The Nov/Dec 2002 issue of Biblical Archaeology Review reported that the ossuary (bone box) of James the Just may have been found in Jerusalem. The engraving on the ossuary says "James, son of Joseph, brother of Jesus". This is significant because only a handful of people

---

92 *The Nicene and Post-Nicene Fathers Second Series, Volume 1*, by Philip Schaff, editor

in Jerusalem at the time could have been "James, son of Joseph, brother of Jesus". One factor that could lead to concluding that the "Jesus" mentioned on the ossuary was indeed the Jesus of the New Testament is that it was unusual at the time to list the brother of the person whose bones were in an ossuary. Like in Josephus, it could have been included to better identify the bones by a more-famous brother.

Tests have shown that the box and at least the first part of the engraving date to c. 63 A.D. However, some scholars, including the Israel Antiquities Authority, have contended that the "brother of Jesus" part of the engraving was added by a forger. However, the IAA was not able to prove their assertion of forgery in a recent trial in Israel.

If this is the ossuary of James the Just, it is the oldest historical or archaeological evidence of the existence of Jesus

Chapter Sixteen – Matthias

Matthias is the most elusive of all the apostles, as his name is mentioned only twice in the New Testament. Matthias was chosen by the Apostles to replace Judas Iscariot, after the death of Judas in the Field of Blood. Matthias was chosen partly by election, and partly by chance:

> So they proposed two men: Joseph called Barsabbas (also known as Justus) and Matthias. Then they prayed, "Lord, you know everyone's heart. Show us which of these two you have chosen to take over this apostolic ministry, which Judas left to go where he belongs." Then they cast lots, and the lot fell to Matthias; so he was added to the eleven apostles. (Acts 1:23-26, NIV)

About all we can say for sure about Matthias is that he was one of the disciples of Jesus from the beginning (probably one of the 'Seventy"), according to the criteria for apostleship set forth by Peter:

> Therefore it is necessary to choose one of the men who have been with us the whole time the Lord Jesus went in and out among us, beginning from John's baptism to the time when Jesus was taken up from us. For one of these must become a witness with us of his resurrection. (Acts 1:21-22, NIV)

Church tradition

According to Hippolytus, Matthias preached in Jerusalem, and died there:

> And Matthias, who was one of the seventy, was numbered along with the eleven apostles, and preached in Jerusalem, and fell asleep and was buried there. (*On the Twelve Apostles*, Hippolytus, Translated by A. Cleveland Coxe, D.D.[93])

Eusebius, in his Church History, numbers Matthias among the Seventy:

> Matthias, also, who was numbered with the apostles in the place of Judas, and the one who was honored by being made a candidate with

---

93 *The Ante-Nicene Fathers Volume 5*, Edited by A. Roberts and J Donaldson

him, are like-wise said to have been deemed worthy of the same call-ing with the seventy. (*The Church History of Eusebius*, Translated By the Rev. Arthur Cushman Mcgiffert, Ph.D., Book 1, Chapter 12[94])

Eusebius, in a discussion regarding the Nicolaitans, records a tradition that Matthias was especially strong at combating the desires of the flesh:

But they say that Matthias also taught in the same manner that we ought to fight against and abuse the flesh, and not give way to it for the sake of pleasure, but strengthen the soul by faith and knowledge. (*The Church History of Eusebius*, Translated By the Rev. Arthur Cush-man Mcgiffert, Ph.D., Book 3, Chapter 29[95])

Intriguingly, Eusebius lists Matthias as one of the 15 bishops of Jerus-alem:

The first, then, was James, the so-called brother of the Lord; the second, Symeon; the third, Justus; the fourth, Zacchaeus; the fifth, To-bias; the sixth, Benjamin; the seventh, John; the eighth, **Matthias**; the ninth, Philip; the tenth, Seneca; the eleventh, Justus; the twelfth, Levi; the thirteenth, Ephres; the fourteenth, Joseph; and finally the fif-teenth, Judas. These are the bishops of Jerusalem that lived between the age of the apostles and the time referred to, all of them belonging to the circumcision. (*The Church History of Eusebius*, Translated By the Rev. Arthur Cushman Mcgiffert, Ph.D., Book 4, Chapter 4; emphas-is added[96])

Apocryphal

Matthias appears in the apocryphal *Acts Of Andrew And Matthias In The City Of The Man-Eaters*. In this tale, he is chosen by lot for the dubious honor of being a missionary among a group of cannibals:

About that time all the apostles had come together to the same place, and shared among themselves the countries, casting lots, in order that each might go away into the part that had fallen to him. By lot, then, it fell to Matthias to set out to the country of the man-eaters. And the men of that city used neither to eat bread nor drink wine; but

---

94 *The Nicene and Post-Nicene Fathers Second Series, Volume 1*, by Philip Schaff, editor
95 *Ibid*
96 *Ibid*

they ate the flesh of men, and drank their blood. Every man, therefore, who came into their city they laid hold of, and digging they
thrust out his eyes, and gave him a drug to drink, prepared by sorcery
and magic; and from drinking the drug his heart was altered and his
mind deranged. (*Acts Of Andrew And Matthias In The City Of The
Man-Eaters*, Translated By Alexander Walker, Esq.[97])

Matthias is captured and tortured by the cannibals, but receives a
revelation from Jesus that the Apostle Andrew will rescue him in 27
days. Right on time, a reluctant Andrew rescues Matthias, and Matthias is miraculously transported into the presence of Peter:

And there were in all two hundred and seventy men and forty-nine
women whom Andrew released from the prison. And the men went
as the blessed Andrew said to them; and he made Matthias go along
with his disciples out of the eastern gate of the city. And Andrew com-
manded a cloud, and the cloud took up Matthias and the disciples of
Andrew; and the cloud set them down on the mountain where Peter
was teaching, and they remained beside him. (*Acts Of Andrew And
Matthias In The City Of The Man-Eaters*, Translated By Alexander
Walker, Esq.[98])

Other traditions place Matthias in Ethiopia.

---

97 *The Ante-Nicene Fathers Volume 8*, Edited by A. Roberts and J Donaldson
98 *Ibid*

Chapter Seventeen – Paul

Paul[99]

> I have fought the good fight, I have finished the race, I have kept the faith. Now there is in store for me the crown of righteousness, which the Lord, the righteous Judge, will award to me on that day—and not only to me, but also to all who have longed for his appearing. (2 Thessalonians 4:6-8, NIV)

The greatest evangelist and theologian of the early church was Paul of Tarsus. Paul was a Hellenized Jew, growing up in a town in Cilicia (Acts 22:3 – Cilicia is in modern day Turkey). The Bible is silent on the year of his birth – various Bible scholars view that it was sometime in the 0-10 A.D. time frame.

Paul received his training under the pre-eminent Rabbi Gamaliel (Acts 22:3), and viewed himself as a "Hebrew of Hebrews":

> ...circumcised on the eighth day, of the people of Israel, of the tribe of Benjamin, a Hebrew of Hebrews; in regard to the law, a Pharisee... (Philemon 3:3, NIV)

Paul's given Hebrew name, Saul, may have been after King Saul, also from the tribe of Benjamin.

It was probably because of the confluence of Greek, Roman and Hebrew influences that Paul experienced in the cosmopolitan city of Tarsus that made Paul such an effective evangelist in his lifetime charge – to bring the hope of Christ to the Gentiles. This charge is referred many times in the New Testament.

> ...the grace God gave me to be a minister of Christ Jesus to the Gentiles with the priestly duty of proclaiming the gospel of God, so that the Gentiles might become an offering acceptable to God, sanctified by the Holy Spirit. (Romans 15:15, NIV)

> I am talking to you Gentiles. Inasmuch as I am the apostle to the Gentiles, I make much of my ministry in the hope that I may somehow arouse my own people to envy and save some of them. (Romans 11:13-14, NIV)

However, Paul's earliest relationship with Christians was in the role of a persecutor, and perhaps, even a hit man for the Sanhedrin. When Stephen is stoned to death, we are told, "And Saul was there, giving approval to his death." (Acts 8:1, NIV) Two verses later, we're told, "Saul began to destroy the church. Going from house to house, he dragged off men and women and put them in prison." (Acts 9:3, NIV)

The journey of Paul from being a great persecutor of Christians to being their most staunch evangelist and supporter happened one day on the road to Damascus, Syria, where Paul had been sent by the Jerusalem high priests to persecute the nascent Christian congregation there. The story of Paul's conversion is considered so important that it is repeated no less than three times in Acts! (Acts 9, 22, 26) It is probably the single most important event in the history of the early Christian Church, ranking with the conversion of Constantine in terms of its long-term consequences.

> On one of these journeys I was going to Damascus with the authority and commission of the chief priests. About noon, O king, as I was on the road, I saw a light from heaven, brighter than the sun, blazing

around me and my companions. We all fell to the ground, and I heard a voice saying to me in Aramaic, "Saul, Saul, why do you persecute me? It is hard for you to kick against the goads." Then I asked, "Who are you, Lord?"' "I am Jesus, whom you are persecuting,"' the Lord replied. "Now get up and stand on your feet. I have appeared to you to appoint you as a servant and as a witness of what you have seen of me and what I will show you. I will rescue you from your own people and from the Gentiles. I am sending you to them to open their eyes and turn them from darkness to light, and from the power of Satan to God, so that they may receive forgiveness of sins and a place among those who are sanctified by faith in me." (Acts 26:12-18, NIV)

After this amazing conversion experience, Paul is ready to spread the word of Jesus throughout the world. However, knowing his reputation as a persecutor of Christians, the apostles in Jerusalem are slow to accept Paul as a convert. It takes the sponsorship of Barnabas (Acts 9:26-27) to eventually ameliorate the concerns of the apostles, although Paul remains the "odd man out" vis-à-vis the rest of the apostles throughout the rest of his ministry (see "Character and Characteristics" section.)

The stage is set for Paul's missionary journeys.

The missionary journeys

The three missionary journeys of Paul (which combined, were over 6,000 miles in length!) effectively spread the word of Christianity throughout the Greco-Roman world.

Paul followed a general pattern when he'd go into a new town. First, he'd preach at the local Jewish synagogue – often to attract Gentile "God-fearers", who believed in the God of Abraham, but hadn't accepted the rigors of Mosaic Law. Next, he would often try to create small churches in the homes of new followers (Lydia and her household, for example, are baptized in Lydia's home). Then in some instances, he would preach in more public arenas (Mars Hill in Athens, for example).

Steps to Mars Hill (Photo by Debra Kasson-Jones)

The following tables summarize the geography and key points of Paul's missionary journeys.

1st Missionary Journey c. 46-48 A.D. (with Barnabas)		
Reference	Notes	Verse(s)
Antioch (Syria), Selucia to Salamis (Cyprus)	Led by the Holy Sprit	Acts 13:1-3
On Cyprus to Paphos	Sorcerer Bar-Jesus blinded by Paul	Acts 13:6-12
Perga in Pamphilia	John Mark leaves	Acts 13:13
Antioch in Pisidia	• In modern-day Turkey • Paul & Barnabas expelled from the region	Acts 13:14-50
Iconium	Plot to stone Paul & Barnabas	Acts 13:51-14:5
Lystra	• Paul heals a	Acts 14:6-20

83

1st Missionary Journey c. 46-48 A.D. (with Barnabas)		
Reference	Notes	Verse(s)
	crippled man • Paul mistaken for Hermes (!) • Paul stoned and left for dead	
Derbe		Acts 14:20-21
Lystra, Iconium, Antioch	Elders appointed in the local churches	Acts 14:21-23
Pisidia, Pamphylia, then Perga		Acts 14:24-25
Attalia		Acts 14:25-26
Antioch (Syria)		Acts 14:26-28

2nd Missionary Journey c. 49-52 (with Silas)		
Reference	Notes	Verse(s)
Syria and Cilicia		Acts 15:41
Derbe and Lystra	Timothy joins Paul	Acts 16:1-5
Phrygia and Galatia		Acts 16:6
Near Mysia, Bithynia	Prevented from entering by the Spirit of Jesus	Acts 16:7
Troas, Samothrace, Neapolis	Paul has a dream in Troas that leads him to Macedonia	Acts 16:8-11
Philippi	• Lydia baptized by Paul • Paul exorcises a demon • Paul and Silas imprisoned; an earthquake shakes the foundations of the jail	Acts 16:12-40
Through Amphipolis and Apollonia to Thessalonica	Paul's preaching incites mob violence	Acts 17:1-9
Berea		Acts 17:10-13
Athens	Paul debates with stoics and Epicureans at the Areopagus (Mars Hill)	Acts 17:14-34

2nd Missionary Journey c. 49-52 (with Silas)		
Reference	Notes	Verse(s)
Corinth	• Paul links up with Priscilla and Aquila; works as a tent-maker • Stays for 1.5 years	Acts 18:1-17
Cenchrea	Paul the Nazorite?	Acts 18:18
Ephesus		Acts 18:19-21
Caesarea, Jerusalem, & Antioch (Syria)		Acts 18:22

When Paul preached on Mars Hill, he was preaching in the center of pagan worship. The nearby Acropolis contains several temples to pagan Gods. The Erechtheion, for example, is devoted to Athena and Poseidon. (Photo by Debra Kasson-Jones)

3rd Missionary Journey c. 53-57 A.D.		
Reference	Notes	Verse(s)
Galatia and Phrygia		Acts 18:23
Ephesus	• 2 year stay • Paul heals the sick	Acts 19:1-41
Macedonia		Acts 20:1-2
Greece, Macedonia, Philippi		Acts 20:3-6
Troas	Paul raises Eutychus from the dead	Acts 20:6-12

3rd Missionary Journey c. 53-57 A.D.		
Reference	Notes	Verse(s)
Assos		Acts 20:13-14
Mitylene, Kios, Samos, Miletus	Paul calls the Ephesian elders to Miletus	Acts 20:14-38
Cos, Rhodes, Patara		Acts 21:1-2
Tyre		Acts 21:3-6
Ptolemais		Acts 21:7
Caesarea	• Paul stays with Philip the evangelist • Paul warned not to go to Jerusalem	Acts 21:9-15
Jerusalem	Paul arrested	Acts 21:16-25

After the completion of Paul's three missionary journeys, the next four years of Paul's life would be spent primarily in jail. First, Paul spent two years in jail in Caesarea under the control of Roman procurators Felix and Festus. Later, he would spend two years in a Roman jail, and write some of his most famous letters, including Colossians and Ephesians.

Paul was arrested in Jerusalem, where he was accused by "some Jews from the province of Asia" of defiling the temple by bringing Greeks (Gentiles) into it. While he briefly appeared before the Sanhedrin (where he skillfully separated the Pharisees and Sadducees by bringing up the doctrine of resurrection of the dead), Paul used his Roman citizenship to claim Roman protection. He was tried before Felix, and seemed to successfully refute the charge of defiling the Temple. However, he would remain in a Roman jail in Caesarea for two years, assumedly as a sop from Felix to the Sanhedrin.

The new pro-curator, Festus, was ready to try the case again, but Paul balked when Festus wanted him to return to Jerusalem for the trial. Paul invoked his right as a Roman citizen to have his case heard by the emperor in Rome. During the long voyage to Rome, Paul would suffer a shipwreck off the coast of Crete.

When Paul arrived in Rome (c. 61 A.D.), according to Acts he interacted with a group of Jews who apparently had heard of Christians, but were not Christians themselves:

> But we want to hear what your [Paul's] views are, for we know that people everywhere are talking against this sect. (Acts 28:18, NIV)

Thus, one could theorize that it was Paul, not Peter, who was the first apostle to reach Rome, and establish the subsequent church.

The account of Paul's travel to Rome ends rather abruptly in Acts (in fact, some scholars believe that Acts was written as Paul's defense before the emperor):

> For two whole years Paul stayed there in his own rented house and welcomed all who came to see him. Boldly and without hindrance he preached the kingdom of God and taught about the Lord Jesus Christ. (Acts 28:30-31, NIV)

So, was Paul tried before Nero and acquitted? Or is this when he met his death? We can only surmise, based on brief references in some of Paul's letters (see, for example, Philemon 1:22), and later church tradition. Most scholars believed that Paul was released from house arrest in Rome in c. 62 A.D., and that he may have made a fourth missionary journey, which may have gone as far as Spain (Rom 15:24, 28). Church tradition says that Nero executed Paul in Rome c. 67 A.D. (see "Church Tradition" section below). However, the New Testament is silent on the death of this great apostle.

Relationship of Peter with Paul

The New Testament records that Peter and Paul, the two greatest apostles of the Early Church, did have some interaction with each other. Galatians 1:18, for example, records that Paul stayed with Peter in Jerusalem for a period of 15 days. Peter supported Paul's ministry to the Gentiles at the Jerusalem Council in Acts 15. This is further supported in Galatians 2:7-10, when Peter (a "pillar") is depicted as supporting Paul's ministry to the Gentiles.

There were some disagreements between the two. In Galatians, 2:11-14 Paul describes an argument that he had with Peter in Antioch.

In 2 Peter 3:15-16, Peter describes that Paul's letters are "hard to understand", but ascribes to them the same authority as the Jewish Scriptures:

> Bear in mind that our Lord's patience means salvation, just as our dear brother Paul also wrote you with the wisdom that God gave him. He writes the same way in all his letters, speaking in them of these matters. His letters contain some things that are hard to understand, which ignorant and unstable people distort, **as they do the other Scriptures**, to their own destruction. (2 Peter 3:15-16, NIV; emphasis added)

Character and characteristics

How does one describe Paul? Some words we might use would be dogged, indefatigable, brave, self-effacing, defensive, logical, persuasive, self-sufficient and (somewhat surprisingly) – humorous. We'll examine some of these strains below.

Dogged, indefatigable, brave

As Paul's description below of his own trials and tribulations as a missionary indicate, he faced remarkable obstacles to his ministry – and yet, he preached throughout the Roman world for three decades! Nothing could stop him, except death at the hands of Nero. Even being thrown in jail didn't stop him – he just used the time to convert his jailers, or to write great theological letters to the churches that he'd started.

> I have worked much harder, been in prison more frequently, been flogged more severely, and been exposed to death again and again. Five times I received from the Jews the forty lashes minus one. Three times I was beaten with rods, once I was stoned, three times I was shipwrecked, I spent a night and a day in the open sea, I have been constantly on the move. I have been in danger from rivers, in danger from bandits, in danger from my own countrymen, in danger from Gentiles; in danger in the city, in danger in the country, in danger at sea; and in danger from false brothers. I have labored and toiled and have often gone without sleep; I have known hunger and thirst and

have often gone without food; I have been cold and naked. Besides everything else, I face daily the pressure of my concern for all the churches. Who is weak, and I do not feel weak? Who is led into sin, and I do not inwardly burn? (2 Corinthians 11:23-29, NIV)

We are hard pressed on every side, but not crushed; perplexed, but not in despair; persecuted, but not abandoned; struck down, but not destroyed. We always carry around in our body the death of Jesus, so that the life of Jesus may also be revealed in our body. (2 Corinthians 4:8-10, NIV)

Self-effacing

Paul - in keeping with his basic theological message that no one is worthy of salvation, and can only be saved through the Grace of God, through faith in Jesus Christ – was the first to admit that he himself was a wretched sinner. No "holier than though" expressions from Paul!

So I find this law at work: When I want to do good, evil is right there with me. For in my inner being I delight in God's law; but I see another law at work in the members of my body, waging war against the law of my mind and making me a prisoner of the law of sin at work within my members. What a wretched man I am! Who will rescue me from this body of death? Thanks be to God—through Jesus Christ our Lord! So then, I myself in my mind am a slave to God's law, but in the sinful nature a slave to the law of sin. (Romans 7:21-25, NIV)

Paul even admits in his letters that he has a particular "thorn in my flesh" with which he must constantly battle. What is the thorn? Paul never says. Malaria? Temptation? Epilepsy? Gluttony?

To keep me from becoming conceited because of these surpassingly great revelations, there was given me a thorn in my flesh, a messenger of Satan, to torment me. Three times I pleaded with the Lord to take it away from me. But he said to me, "My grace is sufficient for you, for my power is made perfect in weakness." Therefore I will boast all the more gladly about my weaknesses, so that Christ's power may rest on me. That is why, for Christ's sake, I delight in weaknesses, in insults, in hardships, in persecutions, in difficulties. For when I am weak, then I am strong. (1 Corinthians 12:7-10, NIV)

Defensive

As mentioned in an earlier section, Paul was a bit of an "odd man out" vis-à-vis the other apostles. Paul had trouble being accepted for several reasons, including:

- He was not one of the original apostles chosen by Jesus during his earthly ministry
- He wasn't a Galilean fisherman – he was from the more cosmopolitan Tarsus in Cilicia
- As a Hellenized Jew, he had been much more exposed to Greek philosophical thought than most of the other apostles
- He started out as a persecutor of the early Christians – perhaps even participating in the stoning of Stephen

As a result of Paul being "different" from the other apostles ("The Twelve"), he sometimes could be a little defensive in his letters:

- In the first sentence of nine of his letters, Paul identifies himself as an Apostle
- Twice in 2 Corinthians, he makes a statement that he is not inferior to so-called "super apostles" (2 Cor 11:5, 12:11)
- In a discussion of one of his trips to Jerusalem, he states, "As for those who seemed to be important—whatever they were makes no difference to me; God does not judge by external appearance —those men added nothing to my message." (Gal 2:6, NIV)
- In referring to James (possibly the brother of Jesus), Peter and John, he calls them "reputed" to be pillars in the church:

> James, Peter and John, those reputed to be pillars, gave me and Barnabas the right hand of fellowship when they recognized the grace given to me. (Galatians 2:9, NIV)

Logical

Until St. Augustine in the late 4th/early 5th century, Paul's letters (especially Romans) formed the most complete theology in the Christian faith. His letters are key source documents for Christian beliefs such as the total wickedness of man, justification by faith, salvation by the Grace of God through faith in Jesus Christ, and communion.

He was able to more than hold his own against various Greek philosophical adherents who debated with him at various points in his ministry (in Athens, for example).

Persuasive

Although Paul himself said that he had poor penmanship (Gal 6:11) and no training as a public speaker (2 Cor 11:6), he must have been remarkably persuasive, to have personally established so many churches through the Greco-Roman world in three decades of ministry.

Paul even shared (in 1 Corinthians) his basic plan for making converts. It sounds amazingly like a marketing plan that might be used by modern day corporations!

> Though I am free and belong to no man, I make myself a slave to everyone, to win as many as possible. To the Jews I became like a Jew, to win the Jews. To those under the law I became like one under the law (though I myself am not under the law), so as to win those under the law. To those not having the law I became like one not having the law (though I am not free from God's law but am under Christ's law), so as to win those not having the law. To the weak I became weak, to win the weak. I have become all things to all men so that by all possible means I might save some. I do all this for the sake of the gospel, that I may share in its blessings. (1 Corinthains 9:19-23, NIV)

Self-sufficient

While Paul had great compassion for those that couldn't help themselves, he was strongly opposed to people who didn't take their fair share of the load. He even insisted on working to pay his fair share of room and board while he was establishing churches throughout the Mediterranean.

> In the name of the Lord Jesus Christ, we command you, brothers, to keep away from every brother who is idle and does not live according to the teaching you received from us. For you yourselves know how you ought to follow our example. We were not idle when we were

with you, nor did we eat anyone's food without paying for it. On the contrary, we worked night and day, laboring and toiling so that we would not be a burden to any of you. We did this, not because we do not have the right to such help, but in order to make ourselves a model for you to follow. For even when we were with you, we gave you this rule: "If a man will not work, he shall not eat." (2 Thessalonians 3:6-10, NIV)

Humor

While humor might be one of the more minor characteristics that we'd apply to Paul, it does show up from time to time. Perhaps the most famous example is in Galatians when Paul, who is fulminating against those that say that Gentile converts must be circumcised, says the following:

> As for those agitators, I wish they would go the whole way and emasculate themselves! (Galatians 5:2-12, NIV)

Church Tradition

Some 25% of the New Testament is made up of letters from Paul to various churches (in Rome, Ephesus, etc.) and to various colleagues (Timothy, Titus, etc.). Pauline authorship was accepted for fourteen letters in the New Testament by the Early Church Fathers, with the possible exception of Hebrews (about which Origen said "God only knows" who wrote it).

> Paul's fourteen epistles are well known and undisputed. It is not indeed right to overlook the fact that some have rejected the Epistle to the Hebrews, saying that it is disputed by the church of Rome, on the ground that it was not written by Paul. But what has been said concerning this epistle by those who lived before our time I shall quote in the proper place. In regard to the so-called Acts of Paul, I have not found them among the undisputed writings. (*The Church History of Eusebius*, Translated By the Rev. Arthur Cushman Mcgiffert, Ph.D., Book 3, Chapter 3[100])

Some modern Biblical scholars doubt that Paul actually wrote the Pastoral letters (1 & 2 Timothy, Titus).

---

100 *The Nicene and Post-Nicene Fathers Second Series, Volume 1,* by Philip Schaff, editor

Hippolytus records that Paul was beheaded in Rome by Nero, after preaching as far afield as Spain:

> And Paul entered into the apostleship a year after the assumption of Christ; and beginning at Jerusalem, he advanced as far as Illyricum, and Italy, and Spain, preaching the Gospel for thirty-five years. And in the time of Nero he was beheaded at Rome, and was buried there. (*On the Twelve Apostles*, Hippolytus, Translated by A. Cleveland Coxe, D.D.[101])

Eusebius also records that Paul was put to death under Nero in Rome:

> It is, therefore, recorded that Paul was beheaded in Rome itself, and that Peter likewise was crucified under Nero. This account of Peter and Paul is substantiated by the fact that their names are preserved in the cemeteries of that place even to the present day. It is confirmed likewise by Caius, a member of the Church, who arose under Zephyrinus, bishop of Rome. He, in a published disputation with Proclus, the leader of the Phrygian heresy, speaks as follows concerning the places where the sacred corpses of the aforesaid apostles are laid: "But I can show the trophies of the apostles. For if you will go to the Vatican or to the Ostian way, you will find the trophies of those who laid the foundations of this church." And that they both suffered martyrdom at the same time is stated by Dionysius, bishop of Corinth, in his epistle to the Romans, in the following words: "You have thus by such an admonition bound together the planting of Peter and of Paul at Rome and Corinth. For both of them planted and likewise taught us in our Corinth. And they taught together in like manner in Italy, and suffered martyrdom at the same time." I have quoted these things in order that the truth of the history might be still more confirmed. (*The Church History of Eusebius*, Translated By the Rev. Arthur Cushman Mcgiffert, Ph.D., Book 2, Chapter 25[102])

Apocryphal

The apocryphal *Acts of Paul and Thecla* (which is much more focused on Thecla than Paul) gives the only known early description of Paul's appearance:

---

101 *The Ante-Nicene Fathers Volume 5*, Edited by A. Roberts and J Donaldson
102 *The Nicene and Post-Nicene Fathers Second Series, Volume 1*, by Philip Schaff, editor

And he saw Paul coming, a man small in size, bald-headed, bandy-legged, well-built, with eyebrows meeting, rather long-nosed, full of grace. For sometimes he seemed like a man, and sometimes he had the countenance of an angel. (*Acts of Paul and Thecla*, Translated By Alexander Walker, Esq.[103])

The *Acts Of The Holy Apostles Peter And Paul* describes the battle in Rome between Paul (and Peter) and Simon the Magician. The battle eventually plays out in front of Nero, and all three (Peter, Paul, Simon) end up dying. The death and burial of Paul is described thus:

Then both Peter and Paul were led away from the presence of Nero. And Paul was beheaded on the Ostesian road. (*Acts Of The Holy Apostles Peter And Paul*, Translated By Alexander Walker, Esq.[104])

Revelation of Paul

Finally, the *Revelation of Paul* builds on the reference in 2 Corinthians 12 to Paul's experiences in the "third heaven". The work begins with these words:

REVELATION of the holy Apostle Paul: the things which were revealed to him when he went up even to the third heaven, and was caught up into paradise, and heard unspeakable words. (*Revelation of Paul*, Translated By Alexander Walker, Esq.[105])

With its emphasis on a well-defined church leadership hierarchy (deacons, bishops, presbyters), we can guess a no-earlier than 2nd or 3rd century date for authorship. St. Augustine thought dimly of this work.

In the course of the vision, Paul receives a tour of heaven, and meets many famous Old Testament characters, including Enoch, Abraham, Isaac, Jacob, David, Manasseh, Joseph, Jeremiah, Ezekiel, Isaiah, Noah and Elias. Paul also meets Mary, mother of Jesus, and the infants slain by King Herod.

---

103 *The Ante-Nicene Fathers Volume 8*, Edited by A. Roberts and J Donaldson
104 *Ibid*
105 *Ibid*

In the course of his tour, Paul describes heaven, the heavenly Jerusalem (compare with Revelation 21) and Paradise – the place from which Adam and Eve were ejected.

Follow me, that I may bring thee into the city of God, and into its light. And its light was greater than the light of the world, and greater than gold, and walls encircled it. And the length and the breadth of it were a hundred stadia. And I saw twelve gates, exceedingly ornamented, leading into the city; and four rivers encircled it, flowing with milk, and honey, and oil, and wine...

And I looked, and saw in the midst of the city an altar, great and very lofty; and there was one standing near the altar, whose face shone like the sun, and he had in his hands a psaltery and a harp, and he sung the Alleluia delightfully, and his voice filled all the city. And all with one consent accompanied him, so that the city was shaken by their shouting. And I asked the angel: Who is this that singeth delightfully, whom all accompany? And he said to me: This is the prophet David; this is the heavenly Jerusalem. When, therefore, Christ shall come in His second appearing, David himself goes forth with all the saints. For as it is in the heavens, so also upon earth...

...And he took me by an impulse of the Spirit, and brought me into paradise. And he says to me: This is paradise, where Adam and Eve transgressed. And I saw there a beautiful tree of great size, on which the Holy Spirit, rested; and from the root of it there came forth all manner of most sweet-smelling water, parting into four channels... And having again taken hold of me by the hand, he led me near the tree of the knowledge of good and evil. And he says to me: This is the tree by means of which death came into the world, and Adam took of the fruit of it from his wife, and ate; and thereafter they were cast out hence. And he showed me another, the tree of life, and said to me: This the cherubim and the flaming sword guard. And when I was closely observing the tree, and wondering, I saw a woman coming from afar off, and a multitude of angels singing praises to her. And I asked the angel: Who is this, my Lord, who is in so great honor and beauty? And the angel says to me: This is the holy Mary, the mother of the Lord. (*Revelation of Paul*, Translated By Alexander Walker, Esq.[106])

---

106 *Ibid*

Chapter Eighteen - Jesus the apostle and high priest

For completeness sake, I should mention that there is one other apostle mentioned outside of the Gospels in the New Testament:

> Therefore, holy brothers, who share in the heavenly calling, fix your thoughts on Jesus, the apostle and high priest whom we confess. (Hebrews 3:1, NIV)

Jesus, the apostle and high priest (Photo by Robert Jones)[107]

Appendix: Leadership in the Early Church

The early church was extremely egalitarian in nature. Every baptized member was seen to have a gift (see Romans 12:4-8, 1 Peter 4:10-11, 1 Corinthians 12:1-31, 1 Corinthians 14:26, Ephesians 4:11-13). But in time, some formal positions of church leadership evolved, probably because of the ever-increasing size of the congregations. Congregations are exhorted several times in the New Testament to obey and submit to their leaders:

> Obey your leaders and submit to their authority. They keep watch over you as men who must give an account. (Hebrews 13:17, NIV; see also 1 Thessalonians 5:12-13 and 1 Timothy 5:17)

The late-first century *First Epistle of Clement to the Corinthians* (probably written by Clement, Bishop of Rome) discusses a line of succession in the churches that was established by the apostles themselves:

> The Apostles have preached to us from the Lord Jesus Christ; Jesus Christ from God...And thus preaching through countries and cities, they appointed the first fruits of their conversion to be bishops and ministers over such as should afterwards believe, having first proved them by the Spirit...So likewise our Apostles knew by our Lord Jesus Christ, that there should contentions arise, upon account of the ministry. And therefore having a prefect fore-knowledge of this, they appointed persons, as we have before said, and then gave direction, how, when they should die, other chosen and approved men should succeed in their ministry. (*First Epistle of Clement to the Corinthians*, Translated by A. Cleveland Coxe, D.D., Chapter 42[108])

We discuss the different "church officials" that appeared in the first century church below.

Apostles

The first custodians of the early church were the apostles – and more specifically, the "The Twelve" chosen by Jesus. The word "apostle" comes from the Greek word *apostolos* that means:

---

108 *The Ante-Nicene Fathers Volume 1*, Edited by A. Roberts and J Donaldson

a *delegate*; specifically an ambassador of the Gospel; officially a *commissioner* of Christ ("apostle"), (with miraculous powers):—apostle, messenger, he that is sent. (*Strongs Hebrew and Greek Dictionaries*)

Immediately before his ascension, Christ instructs his remaining 11 apostles to carry on his ministry:

> But you will receive power when the Holy Spirit comes on you; and you will be my witnesses in Jerusalem, and in all Judea and Samaria, and to the ends of the earth. (Acts 1:8, NIV)

After the ascension, the 11 remaining apostles wished to replace Judas Iscariot, and decided that a prime qualification for the replacement apostle was to have participated in the earthly ministry of Jesus from the start:

> Therefore it is necessary to choose one of the men who have been with us the whole time the Lord Jesus went in and out among us, beginning from John's baptism to the time when Jesus was taken up from us. For one of these must become a witness with us of his resurrection. (Acts 1:21-22, NIV)

Matthias (never to be heard from again in the New Testament) is chosen as the Judas-replacement.

However, the original twelve plus Matthias are not the only apostles referred to in the New Testament. Paul & Barnabas (Acts 14:14), Andronicus and Junias (Romans 16:7) and, possibly, James the brother of Jesus (Galatians 1:19) also receive the appellation. However, no one after the first century used the title.

The reference to Junias as an apostle in Romans 16:7 is interesting because Junias is the feminine form of a Greek name (see below). Depending on how one interprets the passage (is it saying that Andronicus and Junias are well known to the apostles, or that they are outstanding apostles?), we may have grounds to identify a female apostle.

Greet Andronicus and Junias, my relatives who have been in prison with me. They are outstanding among the apostles, and they were in Christ before I was. (Romans 16:7)

Junias (*Iounias*) is clearly of the feminine form, as Thayer's Greek Definitions states:

> 1) a Christian woman at Rome, mentioned by Paul as one of his kinsfolk and fellow prisoners
> Part of Speech: noun proper feminine

Bishop (or overseer)

Next in importance to the apostles were the bishops (or overseers) and the elders. The term bishop comes from the Greek word *episkopos*:

> a superintendent, that is, Christian officer in general charge of a (or the) church (literally or figuratively):—bishop, overseer. (*Strongs Hebrew and Greek Dictionaries*)

In the New Testament, bishops are instructed to be "shepherds of the church of God"

> Keep watch over yourselves and all the flock of which the Holy Spirit has made you overseers. Be shepherds of the church of God, which he bought with his own blood. (Acts 20:28, NIV)

The qualifications to be a bishop are steep:

> Here is a trustworthy saying: If anyone sets his heart on being an overseer, he desires a noble task. Now the overseer must be above reproach, the husband of but one wife, temperate, self-controlled, respectable, hospitable, able to teach, not given to drunkenness, not violent but gentle, not quarrelsome, not a lover of money. He must manage his own family well and see that his children obey him with proper respect. (If anyone does not know how to manage his own family, how can he take care of God's church?) He must not be a recent convert, or he may become conceited and fall under the same judgment as the devil. He must also have a good reputation with outsiders, so that he will not fall into disgrace and into the devil's trap. (1 Timothy 3:1-7, NIV)

See also Philippians 1:1 and 1 Titus 1:5-9.

By the 2nd century, the role of the bishop was more formalized, with a bishop presiding over a diocese or see. Bishops of churches founded by the apostles were said to be in succession to the apostles (for example – John-Polycarp-Irenaeus).

Elder (or presbyter)

The term "elder" comes from the Greek word *presbuteros*. Both "presbyter" and "priest" are derived from this word. According to Strong's:

> Comparative of presbus (*elderly*); *older*; as noun, a *senior*; specifically an Israelite *Sanhedrist* (also figuratively, member of the celestial council) or Christian "presbyter":—elder (-est), old. (*Strongs Hebrew and Greek Dictionaries*)

The term is used in two different ways in the New Testament, depending upon whether it is used in reference to the Jerusalem Church or the Gentile church. In the former, the concept of elder was modeled after the Old Testament pattern, with elders acting as a decision making council in the Jerusalem church (see Acts 15, Acts 21:17-26). The term as we use it today comes from the Gentile church, and is often used to denote the highest official in a particular church or area:

> Paul and Barnabas appointed elders for them in each church and, with prayer and fasting, committed them to the Lord, in whom they had put their trust. (Acts 14:23)

The qualifications for elders are similar to the aforementioned ones for bishop. In fact, one could read Titus 1:5-9 as indicating that there was no distinction between bishops (overseers) and elders in the 1st century church:

> The reason I left you in Crete was that you might straighten out what was left unfinished and appoint elders in every town, as I directed you. An elder must be blameless, the husband of but one wife, a man whose children believe and are not open to the charge of being wild and disobedient. Since an overseer is entrusted with God's work, he

must be blameless—not overbearing, not quick-tempered, not given to drunkenness, not violent, not pursuing dishonest gain. Rather he must be hospitable, one who loves what is good, who is self-controlled, upright, holy and disciplined. He must hold firmly to the trustworthy message as it has been taught, so that he can encourage others by sound doctrine and refute those who oppose it. (Titus 1:5-9)

See also James 5:14-15, 1 Timothy 4:14, and 1 Peter 5:1-4 for other references to elders.

Adding further confusion to the hierarchy of the first century church (were bishops and elders on the same level?), the apostles sometimes referred to themselves as elders - John refers to himself simply as "the elder" in 2 John 1:1 and 3 John 1:1.

Deacons

Finally, we have the deacons, which comes from the Greek word *diakonos*, often translated as "servant":

> an *attendant*, that is, (generally) a *waiter* (at table or in other menial duties); specifically a Christian *teacher* and *pastor* (technically a *deacon* or *deaconess*):—deacon, minister, servant. (*Strongs Hebrew and Greek Dictionaries*)

Traditionally, the first deacons were seven Hellenistic Jewish Christians chosen by the apostles to assist in the "daily distribution of food" to the poor:

> They chose Stephen, a man full of faith and of the Holy Spirit; also Philip, Procorus, Nicanor, Timon, Parmenas, and Nicolas from Antioch, a convert to Judaism. (Acts 6:5, NIV)

Stephen has the distinction of being the first martyr in the history of the church (his murder being aided and abetted by one Saul of Tarsus).

The qualifications to be a deacon are similar to those of being a bishop or elder – with the distinction that there is no requirement to have the gift of teaching:

Deacons, likewise, are to be men worthy of respect, sincere, not in-dulging in much wine, and not pursuing dishonest gain. They must keep hold of the deep truths of the faith with a clear conscience. They must first be tested; and then if there is nothing against them, let them serve as deacons. In the same way, their wives are to be women worthy of respect, not malicious talkers but temperate and trust-worthy in everything. A deacon must be the husband of but one wife and must manage his children and his household well. Those who have served well gain an excellent standing and great assurance in their faith in Christ Jesus. (1 Timothy 3:8-13, NIV)

By the end of the first century, deacons assisted church leaders, man-aged the church treasury, and served the needs of the poor. In time, they also assisted (but not administered) in sacraments such as bap-tism.

Both women and men served as deacons in the early church, as can be seen by the Phoebe mentioned by Paul in Romans 16:1-2. The NIV translates it as follows:

I commend to you our sister Phoebe, a servant of the church in Cen-chrea. I ask you to receive her in the Lord in a way worthy of the saints and to give her any help she may need from you, for she has been a great help to many people, including me. (Romans 16:1-2, NIV)

The word that the NIV (and KJV) translates as "servant" is actually from the Greek word *diakonos*, defined above (the NIV has a note which gives an alternative translation of *diakonos* as "deaconess").

Women in leadership positions

There is ample evidence that Christianity was an egalitarian religion at its inception – both men and women were welcome in leadership po-sitions. We've already mentioned Phoebe the Deacon, and (possibly) Junias the Apostle. The table below summarizes some of the church leadership positions of women in the New Testament.

Woman	Reference	Comment
Phoebe	Romans 16:1-2	"a deaconess of the church"
Priscilla (or Prisca)	Romans 16:3-5, 1 Cor-	Founded at least two

Woman	Reference	Comment
	inthians 16:19	home churches with her husband Aquila
Junias	Romans 16:7	"outstanding among the apostles"
Nympha	Colossians 4:15	Started a church in her house
Mary, Mother of Jesus	Acts 1:14	Present at first meetings of church
Euodia, Syntyche	Philemon 4:2-3	"these women who have contended at my side in the cause of the gospel"
Four daughters of Philip	Acts 21:8/9	Prophetesses

Sources

Title	Author	Publisher	Date
Ante-Nicene Fathers Volume 1, The	Edited by A. Roberts and J Donaldson	Ages Software	1997
Ante-Nicene Fathers Volume 10, The	Edited by A. Roberts and J Donaldson	Ages Software	1997
Ante-Nicene Fathers Volume 5, The	Edited by A. Roberts and J Donaldson	Ages Software	1997
Ante-Nicene Fathers Volume 8, The	Edited by A. Roberts and J Donaldson	Ages Software	1997
Burial Box of James the Brother of Jesus	André Lemaire	Biblical Archaeology Review	Nov/ Dec 2002
Complete Gospels, The	Robert J. Miller, Editor	Polebridge	1992
Holy Bible - New International Version		Zondervan Publishing House	1973
Life And Works Of Flavius Josephus, The	William Whiston, Translator	Ages Software	1997
Lives of the Saints	Rev. Alban Butler	Gallery Books	1990
Martyrs Mirror	Thieleman J. van Braght	Herald Press	1992
Nicene And Post-Nicene Fathers First Series, Volume 9, The	Philip Schaff, editor	Ages Software	1996, 1997
Nicene And Post-Nicene Fathers Second Series, Vol. 1, The	Philip Schaff, editor	Ages Software	1996, 1997
Oxford Companion to the Bible	Bruce Metzger & Michael Coogan	Oxford University Press	1993
Strongs Hebrew and Greek Dictionaries		Parsons Technology	1999
Thayer's Greek Definitions		Parsons Technology	1999
Who's Who in the Bible	Joan Conway & Ronald Brownrigg	Bonanza Books	1972

About the Author

Robert C. Jones grew up in the Philadelphia, Pennsylvania area. In 1981, he moved to the Atlanta, Georgia area, where he received a B.S. in Computer Science at DeVry Institute of Technology. From 1984-2009, Robert worked for Hewlett-Packard as a computer consultant. He now works as an independent computer support and video services consultant.

Robert is an ordained elder in the Presbyterian Church. He has written and taught numerous adult Sunday School courses. He has also been active in choir ministries over the years, and has taught the Disciples Bible Study six times. He is the author of *A Brief History of Protestantism in the United States* and *Meet the Apostles: Biblical and Legendary Accounts*.

Robert is President of the Kennesaw Historical Society, for whom he has written several books, including *The Law Heard 'Round the World - An Examination of the Kennesaw Gun Law and Its Effects on the Community*, *Retracing the Route of the General - Following in the Footsteps of the Andrews Raid*, and *Images of America: Kennesaw*.

Robert has also written several books on ghost towns in the Southwest, including in Death Valley, Nevada, Arizona, New Mexico, and Mojave National Preserve.

In 2005, Robert co-authored a business-oriented book entitled *Working Virtually: The Challenges of Virtual Teams*.

His interests include the Civil War, Medieval Monasteries, American railroads, ghost towns, hiking in Death Valley and the Mojave, and Biblical Archaeology.

Robert is available as a guest speaker in the Atlanta/North Georgia area (robertcjones@mindspring.com).

Cover: Library of Congress LC-DIG-pga-02626